CW00660580

On the Scent
with Sherlock Holmes

On the Scent with Sherlock Holmes

SOME OLD PROBLEMS RESOLVED

Walter Shepherd

ARTHUR BARKER LIMITED LONDON
A subsidiary of Weidenfeld (Publishers) Limited

Published in Great Britain by
Arthur Barker Limited
91 Clapham High Street
London SW4 7TF

ISBN 0 213 16691 7

Printed in Great Britain by
Bristol Typesetting Co Ltd
Barton Manor, St Philips, Bristol

Contents

Introductory - the Holmes Cult

THERE are nearly a hundred and fifty Sherlock Holmes societies throughout the world. One hundred and twenty-seven of them are in the United States, but there are others in Holland, Denmark, Sweden, Canada, New Zealand, Hong Kong, and England outside London, the home of the parent society.

These societies meet for discussion, to hear papers read, and to debate the results of original research into problems arising, mainly, from Conan Doyle's unguarded inconsistencies, inevitable slips, and sometimes careless errors of fact. The object is to give some plausible explanation for these lapses, or to explain them away, so as to make the life and work of Sherlock Holmes absolutely credible and a suitable foundation for plausible extensions of his 'official' biography.

This is not to deceive anybody, any more than lifelike portraits are painted to deceive anybody, but for the sheer pleasure of overcoming apparently insuperable difficulties by the exercise of ingenuity, and for the healthy conflict of wits in unending debates and battles that are never won. It may all seem very pointless, but it is in its pointlessness that its chief virtue lies. It is gratuitous, inconsequent and unique, and so has the status of independent existence. No doubt psychologists can 'type' Sherlock Holmes with great exactness, yet he is not a recognizable social type in the sense that Mr Pickwick and Bertie Wooster are. He comes out of the blue. His world is a separate universe, overlapping our familiar one at a thousand points so that we are both fascinated and bemused.

For Sherlock Holmes has become just such a legend as Prester John, the Wandering Jew, or the Ancient Mariner, and the labour spent in vindication of the reports of his deeds is exceeded only by that devoted to those of King Arthur. King Arthur, however, is believed to be dead by even his most enthusiastic admirers, whereas there are people who believe that Sherlock Holmes is still alive. The post-bag received at the present 221 Baker Street frequently contains letters from all parts of the world addressed to Sherlock Holmes and requesting his services, in spite of the fact that he would now be 125 years old!

The Sherlock Holmes saga is unique in having no grave or portentous origin, though there may be something of archetypal significance in it. It is a shadowy but felicitous *phenomenon,* with a sevenfold power of attraction. First, it feeds a nostalgia for the romantic, if strenuous, period in which many still lively millions spent their childhood. Second, there is the old-fashioned appeal of stories convincingly displaying the triumph of good over evil. For some, Holmes is the perennial Avenger. Third, there is the human appeal of the characters portrayed in the stories: their hopes, fears, satisfactions, excitements – all conveniently done up in packets of from five to ten thousand words with an extraordinary air of verisimilitude. Fourth, there is the intellectual challenge of Holmes's ingenious 'deductions'. Fifth, the extended development of the legend affords an intellectual amusement of no more serious consequence than that of a crossword puzzle but vastly more rich and entertaining.

The remaining two attractions (and there may be others) are somewhat in the nature of spin-offs. The sixth is that the inventiveness, literary skill and – yes, naïvety – of Conan Doyle himself make the original achievement little short of marvellous, and invite enquiry into the origins of Holmes and Watson and their relations to Doyle's own experiences as revealed in the several available biographies. Seventh, the persons and places involved in the stories are for the most part real, and they are either named or bear thinly disguised cognomens. This has led to astonishingly painstaking researches into local history and, particularly, into the changing scene of the streets and institutions of London during the latter part of the nineteenth century and the early years of the twentieth. The large commentative and well documented literature on Sherlock Holmes has thus made readily available a mass of obscure facts – and old illustrations – of historical interest which would otherwise have remained buried in the archives.

Apart from the books, a great many plays and film-scripts have been produced for the entertainment of the public. Sherlock Holmes has often been lampooned, ridiculed, mocked and caricatured, but none of this frolicking makes the slightest difference to his brooding presence. 'I have no time for trifles,' he once told Dr Watson, and he remains unmoved and unmoveable. And the paradox is that the delighted audiences at these often ludicrous charades consist chiefly of his own devoted followers. At his court, the jesters are as popular and important as the ministers. In fact, everything goes – except the man himself. There never was such a cult as the cult of Sherlock Holmes!

The special Sherlock Holmes section in the St Marylebone Public Library contains more than five hundred books and other publications on or about the great detective and the estimable Dr Watson. The present author cannot claim to have read more than a scantling of this mass of literature and realizes that some of the topics dealt with have been written about many times before by others. He has unwittingly followed the advice given by Sir Edward Bullard in a BBC broadcast in 1963: 'I think it is best to work for a while at a subject before reading what other people have done. If you read other people's papers for several days on end you will get into their way of thinking and may miss ideas that would otherwise have occurred to you.' It is, of course, always possible that even one's most 'original' thoughts will also have occurred to others, but that sort of coincidence may be accepted as additional evidence of plausibility.

The perusal of the 'scantling' referred to above has, nevertheless, given the author much pleasure and inspiration, and provided a sort of challenge to enter the lists. He feels particularly indebted to W. S. Baring-Gould, D. Martin Dakin, Michael Harrison, Ronald A. Knox, Dorothy Sayers and Vincent Starrett. He owes a personal debt to Martin Dakin for introducing him to the Sherlock Holmes Society of London, and for his preliminary inspection of the holograph of the letter from Mr Trample Cloisture, printed in full on pages 101–2. The author also wishes to express his gratitude to Nicholas Utechin for reading and helpfully commenting on this introduction. Finally, acknowledgements are due to the editors of *The Sherlock Holmes*

Journal for permission to incorporate (on pages 98–9) the paragraphs about Barker, which appeared in the author's letter in the summer issue of 1977.

I

On the Scent

In Dr Watson's first description of Sherlock Holmes he remarks that 'his thin, hawk-like nose gave his whole expression an air of alertness and decision.' In his account of the detective's examination of Enoch Drebber's body (also in *A Study in Scarlet*) he says that Holmes 'sniffed the dead man's lips', thus ascertaining that he had taken poison. In *The Naval Treaty* he exclaims, 'Ah, a scent of tobacco would have been worth a great deal to us in such an investigation.' Again, in *The Cardboard Box* he recognized the smell of coffee on a brown-paper wrapping and identified a piece of nautical tarred twine by 'holding it up to the light and sniffing it.' He smelt the tar-like odour of creosote in Bartholomew Sholto's room in *The Sign of Four*, and he sniffed the muzzle of the hound of the Baskervilles, thus establishing that the luminous material was *not* phosphorus.*

The use of the nose in examination has frequently been advocated by other experts, and Sherlock Holmes was by no means the first. For example, Dr Joseph Bell

* When Watson says it is phosphorus, Holmes's remark, 'A cunning preparation of it. There is no smell . . .' must be considered as ironic, if not sarcastic, for even if his chemistry was not as 'profound' as Watson imagined, it was certainly not negligible. See page 30.

of Edinburgh, (who was also noted for his hawk-like beak) is on record as having identified a man's occupation solely by smell. 'This man is a french-polisher,' Dr Bell told his students. 'Come, now! Can't you *smell* him?' In modern times the value of the sense of smell to diagnosis in pathology and forensic science was extolled by Sir Bernard Spilsbury.

When he was called in to conduct the post-mortem on the exhumed body of Edmund Duff, during the investigations into the notorious Croydon poisoning case of 1928–29, he began the proceedings by requesting the other doctor present to clear his nose with a good blow. He then 'secured a strong screwdriver and prised open the lid of the coffin and . . . said, "Give a sniff." This we did simultaneously and, standing up, Spilsbury said one word, "Arsenic". There was no delay, no hesitation, in saying the incriminating word.'*

Holmes was an expert at identification by scent, but for tracking he employed the far more sensitive noses of dogs. For this purpose he seems to have favoured mongrels of curious extraction and unprepossessing appearance. In *The Sign of Four* he employed Toby, 'an ugly, long-haired, lop-eared creature, half spaniel and half lurcher, brown and white in colour, and with a very clumsy, waddling gait.' The scent Toby had to follow in tracking Jonathan Small from Upper Norwood to Mordecai Smith's landing-stage on the Thames was creosote, and he had little difficulty in first tracing the creosote to a damaged barrel in a timber yard. This was a mistake, but not from the dog's point of view, who soon set matters right by back-tracking to a junction of trails.

* From *The Riddle of Birdhurst Rise,* a detailed history and critical review of this case by Richard Whittington-Egan.

When Holmes laid the scent himself, as he did in the case of *The Missing Three-quarter,* he used aniseed and a dog called Pompey. Pompey was a 'squat, lop-eared, white-and-tan dog, something between a beagle and a foxhound', and he was eminently successful in finding Mr Godfrey Staunton. These are the only two detailed accounts we have of Holmes's use of dogs for tracking, but he often seemed to emulate them himself.

Of Holmes's examination of the room in Lauriston Gardens, in *A Study in Scarlet*, Watson writes, 'he trotted noiselessly about the room, sometimes stopping, occasionally kneeling, and once lying flat on his face. . . . As I watched him I was irresistibly reminded of a pure-blooded, well-trained foxhound as it dashes backwards and forwards through the covert, whining in its eagerness, until it comes across the lost scent.' And again, in *The Boscombe Valley Mystery,* Watson says that

> Sherlock Holmes was transformed when he was hot upon such a scent as this. . . . A question or remark . . . only provoked a quick, impatient snarl in reply. Swiftly and silently he made his way along the track. . . . Sometimes Holmes would hurry on, sometimes stop dead, and once he made quite a little *détour* into the meadow. . . . He ran round, like a dog who is picking up a scent. . . . He ran up and down, sometimes losing, sometimes finding the track, until we were . . . under the shadow of a great beech.

Here, he lay down upon his face with a little cry of satisfaction, thus abandoning the dog act right at the critical point.

He was, however, tracking by sight, not by scent, for his hawk-like nose was better suited to qualitative analysis. In this field a trained sense of smell must have been invaluable in the late nineteenth century, for London's inhabitants were then assailed daily by a far greater variety of scents, odours and plain stinks than the modern Londoner can readily imagine. In fact, it was almost impossible in those days to go anywhere in the streets without smelling something, even if it was only a pile of steaming horse manure – which was not thought to be at all unpleasant.

The horse manure was scooped into buckets by large numbers of boys who earned perhaps six shillings a week selling it to gardeners and park-keepers, and enormous piles of rotting manure stood more or less permanently in the 'works' corners of the parks. Another army of boys collected dog's dung, known as 'pure',* from the pavements and curbstones for sale to the tanners of Bermondsey at a shilling a pailful. For this reason, the streets of London were probably freer from defilement by dogs than they are today. We may suppose that a bucket of pure pure standing on the kerb while collection went on smelt more strongly – and certainly more attractively – to the dog population than the human, but complaints were certainly made, especially by people with small children.

Some of the more pleasant scents of the period we no longer experience, and this is, perhaps, a pity in spite of the 'improvements' which have done away with them. For example, on a hot summer's day after a heavy shower, as soon as the sun beat down again on the wet grit roads a quite indescribable odour accompanied the steam which rose from them. This scent

* Pure, so-called, according to Mayhew, because of its use by tanners for purifying the thinner and more delicate skins, such as morocco and calf for bookbinding. It is 'astringent as well as highly alkaline' and is kept 'in pits with an admixture of lime and bark.' The Oxford Dictionary applies the word (as a verb) to the thorough cleansing of the skins 'so as to show one *i.e.*, a pure colour only.' Some writers have spelt the word 'puer', but this is incorrect.

may still be enjoyed in areas where the grit roads survive, and in regions of barren, dusty or clayey earth, *without soil,* as in parts of Australia and the Indian province of Uttar Pradesh. It has recently been the subject of scientific research and its cause is at least partly understood. But to give an account of that would be an unwarrantable digression here.*

Holmes and Watson, and doubtless many of our older readers, were perfectly familiar with this peculiar road scent, but modern road-surfaces are unable to catch it. It was not, however, present in central London or densely built-up areas, where many of the streets were paved with granite setts, cobbles, or wooden blocks soaked in creosote and covered with pitch or tar. Asphalt began to be used in 1871, but though the smells of asphalt and hot tar are still with us they have been much less common since emulsions have been used for waterproofing roads.

Another curious scent for travellers was the penetrating earthy-ozoney smell which pervaded the tunnels and stations of the City and South London tube railway. This was quite distinctive – none of the other Underground lines had quite the same atmosphere though they produced the occasional tang of ozone, as they do

* But a brief footnote may, perhaps, be permitted for curious readers. In short, the scent is now attributed to microscopic traces of an oily or resinous substance absorbed by particles of a clay-like nature in the dust or grit. The aromatic substance appears to come originally from plants of many kinds whose volatile essences are evaporated by hot sunshine and are carried by breezes to the barren areas. The name 'petrichor' has been given to it (in Australia) though its nature is not precisely known. In India, it is actually extracted and sold as a perfume called *Matti ha Attar*. A readily available popular account of it is to be found in Chapter nine of *Butter Side Up*, by Magnus Pyke, published by Watson's own firm of John Murray, 1976. This scent should not be confused with that of wet soil, which is produced by *Leptothrix* and other soil bacteria.

today. The City and South London was the first electric Underground railway and it was opened in 1890, but this was well within the odorous period under review and Holmes and Watson probably sniffed it more than once. The air in the Waterloo and City Railway, opened in 1898, also had a unique earthy smell, though this is not why it is popularly known as 'the Drain' – a nickname referring only to its dimensions.

The 'cut-and-cover' Underground railways, such as the Metropolitan, were steam-driven and began – in 1863 – as very smoky affairs, though perhaps not quite as smoky as some modern writers appear to imagine. The smoky 'trial runs' soon led to the preclusion of locomotives emitting either steam or smoke, chiefly because it interfered with signalling, and the very bad occurrences sometimes described as if they were general were, in fact, exceptional once the special smoke and steam condensers were introduced. The large flexible pipes laid along the sides of the engines from the cylinders and firebox to the tenders, clearly visible in many photographs, belonged to these. Though the *smell* of the smoke was often noticeable this was evidently regarded as less objectionable than that of tobacco smoke, for tobacco smoking was forbidden entirely on the Metropolitan until 1868, when special 'smoking' carriages were introduced.

The popular idea of the smokiness of the old Underground has arisen partly from the exaggerated drawings in contemporary numbers of *Punch* and other illustrated papers, and partly from the fact that when London was blanketed with a 'pea-soup' fog the Underground tunnels were also full of it. At such times it was often impossible to see more than a few inches in front of one's nose and the Underground remained full of the apparent 'smoke' long after the upper air had cleared. Occasionally a completely black fog would descend on the London streets, and such a 'London particular' would bring all outdoor activity to a standstill.*

There was, however, often a smell of ordinary smoke in the London air, especially in the winter, for then all kinds of coal were being burnt in a million fire-places, a thousand factory furnaces, and perhaps a thousand railway engines, to say nothing of the steamers on the river. There was, in fact, no official smoke control above ground and the coal being burnt produced the soot which blackened the white Portland stone of London's churches, government offices and great commercial buildings. It also disseminated sulphurous fumes which were not only irritating to breathe but positively destructive. They attacked the magnesian limestone of which the new Houses of Parliament (opened in 1852) were built, turning it slowly into Epsom salts, which the rain washed away. As a result the houses of Parliament have been in and out of scaffolding ever since, for the

* The author remembers one such fog as late as 1918 (or 1919?) in which it was so black on the streets at mid-day that even the street lamps could not be seen from a distance of more than few yards. A struck match held before the eyes looked like a pale green triangle of luminous paint, and one tried to feel one's way along by touching the walls and shop-fronts but soon gave it up. Only the foolhardy attempted to cross the road in an unfamiliar district – not because of the traffic, which was everywhere at a complete standstill, but because to do so meant getting lost with but a small chance of even finding one's way back to the starting point. This state of affairs lasted about an hour, after which vehicles and pedestrians were able to move at a crawl in a thick yellow atmosphere with a visibility of about eighteen inches, the conductors of the buses walking in front like the obsolete man with the red flag. There have been a few very thick fogs since then but nothing for half a century approaching the real old London blackout, which turned mid-day to moonless midnight with the street lamps apparently replaced by debilitated glow-worms, just visible but throwing no light.

piecemeal replacement of the crumbling rock with a more durable stone.

Other smells on the streets included those caused by defective drains and these became a major nuisance long before Holmes first came to London – a nuisance which was not under reasonably satisfactory control until about 1920. This is not the place to tell the fascinating story of London's sewage problems, or how Sir Joseph Bazalgette's system of 'intercepting' sewers was adopted in 1856, but took twenty years to implement and, by then, proved still inadequate. Nevertheless, an idea of the problems which had to be solved should be given, though the worst of them antedated Holmes's arrival in London.

It should be understood at the outset that the principal job of the sewers is to carry off rainwater, domestic waste water (largely from baths and washing) and industrial waste water. Through the greater part of London's history this was done by ditches or 'kennels' pouring into the eighteen small rivers which flow through London into the Thames. Solid rubbish was often thrown into the rivers but it was properly tipped on to enormous mounds like those owned by Mr Boffin, 'The Golden Dustman', in Dickens's *Our Mutual Friend.* Obnoxious organic waste was chiefly disposed of in hundreds of thousands of cess-pits, though the entrails of animals from the slaughter houses and much other offensive matter was commonly thrown into the rivers also. The rivers were supplemented by deep artificial channels, generally bricked over, called 'sewers', and they took all this filth, including, not infrequently, dead cats, dogs and vermin, into the Thames. But it was not then carried out to sea, as was intended, but was simply washed to and fro' by the tides.

In many districts, such as Bermondsey, it poisoned the drinking water and occasioned widespread outbreaks of cholera. Deaths from cholera in London numbered more than 5,000 in 1832, more than 14,000 in 1849, and more than 10,000 in 1854 (when Sherlock Holmes was one year old). During the 'Great Stink' of 1858 the windows of the Houses of Parliament were hung with curtains soaked in chloride of lime, for the air in the chamber was considered unbreathable. The stench rising from the Thames prevented the members from using the committee rooms and library of the House of Commons at all and, by 1869, the solid sewage had formed banks in the Thames dangerous to shipping. The last cholera epidemic was in 1866 but London's highest death-rate (24·4 per 1,000), attributable chiefly to the drains, was not reached until 1870, after which it slowly declined.

A large part of the main drainage works was, nevertheless, in use by 1865, and when Holmes came to London in 1877 domestic usages were, outwardly, much as they are today, though the smell of bad drains was still too common for ordinary people to do more than give a wry smile in passing. Even the private residences of the nobility and aristocracy were liable to suffer, for the steps taken to combat the evil were constantly being overtaken by the rate of increase of the population. By 1870 London's population had risen to four million and the disposal of 400 million gallons of bad water per day became absolutely necessary. Yet the decision not to allow crude sewage to be discharged into the Thames was not taken until 1884, works for the treatment of sewage were not completed until 1889, and the building of the six sludge ships to take the treated solids out to sea took from 1888 to 1895.

The sewers were ventilated by gratings in the middle of the roads, so that bad smells frequently drifted down the streets. In 1886 this was such a nuisance that a committee recommended periodic cleaning of the sewers and supplying them with more fresh air. In 1898 the gratings were supplemented by pipes running up the sides of buildings to roof level, but the evil was still present in 1914, when sewer-gas exploded in the Post Office telephone ducts. It was again the cause of numerous complaints in the hot summer of 1929, when the experiment of closing six hundred of the sewer ventilators was tried, and in 1930 increased pipe ventilation was again recommended – but this was long after Holmes had left London for Sussex. In some districts the dangerous sewer-gas was trapped and used for lighting the street lamps up above. According to Nicholas Barton, in *The Lost Rivers of London* (1962), the last of these lamps, in Dansey Place off Wardour Street, disappeared 'only recently'.

But this is more than enough on the smell of the drains to indicate what the hawk-like nose had to cope with as a sort of fluctuating background to scents of more practical value. There were, of course, other effluvia of a more local character, such as the appalling stinks round the tanneries of Bermondsey, the knacker's yards, and the glue factories – not to mention Billingsgate. The odours which wafted on the breezes from the breweries and the gas-works were less distressing. Earl Grey had declared that the stench of the gaseous matter floating in the Thames was 'exceedingly dangerous', but the smell of coal-gas was, strangely enough, thought by the common people to be of benefit to the health. Poor mothers who could not afford a doctor would wheel their prams up and down outside the gas-works, hoping thereby to cure their infants of such ailments as whooping cough. This was observed in practice outside Croydon gas-works as late as 1927. In the story called *The Retired Colourman,* Holmes readily distinguished the smell of gas from that of paint and so uncovered a murder.

Another odour thought to be beneficial in some cases was the ammonia often wafted from the stables in the mews. The total quantity of ammonia arising from this source was considerable for London possessed an enormous population of horses, which were the chief source of power for transport of all kinds other than the railways. The bus and tram companies alone employed around 20,000 horses, and it is impossible to estimate the number used by tradesmen, carriers, cabs and private carriages. The army also had several large stables and still more horses came into London from the country daily, bringing vast quantities of meat, vegetables, fruit and other products to the markets.

Until the latter part of the nineteenth century saltpetre, required for making gunpowder and salting meat, was still being manufactured from manure and crude sewage, though the art was fast disappearing as mineral saltpetre began to be imported. The old 'Saltpetre Man' had long since lost his authority to call at all stables to scrape earth from the floors and encrustations from the walls,* and the manufacturers now maintained their own cellars in which the manure and ordure were

* Hence orient Nitre owes its sparkling birth,
And with prismatic crystals gems the earth,
Or frosts with branching plumes the mould'ring walls;
. . . As woos Azotic Gas the virgin Air.

Erasmus Darwin, *The Economy of Vegetation.*

'Nitre' = saltpetre; 'Azotic Gas' = nitrogen.

acted upon by nitrifying bacteria. The appalling smells of sulphuretted hydrogen (rotten eggs) and carbon disulphide (bad drains) escaped mostly through the chimneys, but the unmistakeable pungency of ammonia was often wafted down the streets.

The ammoniacal odour of dirty stables, street latrines, and saltpetre factories, may not have had any real virtue – except, perhaps, as a sort of diluted smelling-salts – but it was certainly not as poisonous as the petrol fumes for which we have exchanged it. Holmes, of course, was familiar with these too. Another smell to do with transport was that of hot engine oil, still beloved of steam railway enthusiasts and remembered nostalgically by passengers in the old paddle-steamers and steam ferry-boats.

There were oil lamps in every house in the 1890s – even in those with gas-light, in case of failure in the supply or the breaking of the last mantle. There were also oil heaters and cookers, and the smell of paraffin was often noticeable. Sometimes it even got into the food, when the cook-general refilled a lamp in the underground kitchen while cooking the dinner. Unnoticed paraffin on her fingers would make everything she touched afterwards taste of it. Street markets were lit by naphtha flares, which had a different though similar smell, and sometimes by acetylene burners, which smelt abominably when being lit or after getting blown out.

A pedestrian in the streets of London was more often enveloped in the delicious aroma of roasting coffee than he is today, though the cheaper brands of coffee were often adulterated to a degree which is now totally illegal. According to the 1876 edition of Chambers's Encyclopaedia, 'Coffee in its powdered form is not merely adulterated with chicory, but additionally with roasted grain, roots, acorns, sawdust, exhausted tan (termed croats), coffina (the seed of a Turkish plant), burnt sugar, and (worst of all) baked horses' and bullocks' liver.' The walker was less often assaulted by hot waves of spiced cooking from Indian restaurants than he is today, but he was just as frequently aware of English, French and Italian cooking, both with and without garlic or onion, though never with fish and chips.

Should he call at a house he would not be surprised to smell mildew, for damp courses had not been introduced and the lower parts of the walls were frequently damp enough to grow moulds. It was for this reason that the front door and ground floor were often up a flight of half a dozen steps, the basement being thought dry enough only for servants. The basement, however, was not the only region where mice might have been smelt, for the house-mouse sensibly preferred the warm dry spaces behind the upstairs skirting-boards, and under the bedroom floors, when it could find a way up.

Even in a 'respectable' street the visitor was occasionally assailed by the sickly, pungent smell of bugs or cockroaches the moment the front door was opened. If so, he would be only mildly surprised, for was there not a firm advertised as 'Tiffin and Son, Bug-destroyers to Her Majesty and the Royal Family'? Holmes would have expected to find bugs in the slum areas, but his investigations rarely took him into the really poor districts, though he knew Upper Swandam Lane, 'east of London Bridge' (Shadwell), and occasionally spent his day 'in long walks, which appeared to take him into the lowest portions of the City'.

He prided himself on his exact knowledge of London and was, of course, familiar with the docks and dockland, on the south bank at least as far east as Rotherhithe (as reported in *The Dying Detective*). But if he ever ventured into a 'thieves' kitchen' or a 'ghetto' he would have been disguised as a sort of Bill Sykes or Fagin, for even the police seldom went into such areas except in pairs and with their hands ready on their truncheons. So it is doubtful if Holmes was familiar with that unique and indescribable stench which Arthur Morrison called 'the odour of the Jago'.* It is true that he occasionally had dealings with roughs and toughs, but though the negro prize-fighter, Steve Dixie, who turned up in the affair of *The Three Gables,* may well have lived in the Old Nichol, we cannot cite as evidence of this the following exchange of words when Holmes 'clapped his hand to his pocket':

'Lookin' for your gun, Masser Holmes?'

'No; for my scent-bottle, Steve.'

'You are funny, Mr Holmes, ain't you?'

In buses, in street crowds, or in the Underground railways, the curious smell of the early mackintoshes was prominent in wet weather, and sweaty bodies in fine. Most people wore too many layers of clothing and were over-heated. There would often be the peculiarly musty smell of old or dirty clothes, too, especially on drizzly days, for clothes were largely of wool and woollen garments like stockings, socks, combinations ('long-johns') and heavy vests were worn everyday for a week or a fortnight before being washed. The smell of dirty socks became a standing schoolboy joke – like 'toenail jam'. Tweeds and flannels were expected to

* *A Child of the Jago,* by Arthur Morrison, 1896 and often reprinted. Morrison's 'Old Jago' would have been known to Holmes as 'The Old Nichol' and Old Nichol Street is still there, near the junction of Shoreditch High Street and Bethnal Green Road. The whole district was, however, cleared up at the turn of the century through the efforts of the Reverend Osborne Jay.

last for several years but, though visible 'spots' were sponged off and they were sometimes pressed, they seldom had a thorough clean in the modern sense.

But everybody had a 'Sunday best' which was kept for exhibiting oneself at church or paying special social calls, and often enough this suit smelt of lavender or the camphor used to keep away moths. (The smell of camphor, incidentally, was not as objectional as the later naphthalene 'moth balls'.) And, for a time even the most respectable ladies wore skirts long enough to sweep the pavements and collect anything dropped by humans or dogs.

There were a vast number of small shops which had their own peculiar odours, too, and a dwindling remnant of these is still with us, though the smells are not quite the same. The grocers are not as spicy as they used to be, the bakers not so doughy, and the butchers not so fleshy. The leather shops, saddlers and boot repairers are much the same, though scarcer, but the oil-and-colourman, with his blended smell of linseed and turpentine, disappeared when the chemical firms took over the production of paints and varnishes. The corn chandler, too, and the smell of sainfoin chaff, seem to have vanished, and while we still have the ironmonger he no longer sells 'loose' methylated spirits, turpentine, linseed oil (boiled and raw), paraffin, tallow or tar.

For some years Holmes and Watson lived in a multi-scented atmosphere of the kind described, and they were familiar with many common household substances whose scents are no longer with us. It is true that we still have carbolic soap in a much refined form, but today we seldom come across a hot, steaming scullery pervaded by its smell. The scent of 'lime cream' hair-dressing, which Holmes recognized in Mr Henry Baker's hat (in *The Blue Carbuncle*), and that of heliotrope brilliantine, were very common up to the First World War, but the hawk-like nose never sniffed lemon-scented washing up liquid, tangerine-scented soap, or banana-flavoured toothpaste.

We no longer burn sulphur in bedrooms lately occupied by persons with infectious diseases, to kill lurking germs with the poisonous choking fumes, and nor is this the modern method of destroying vermin, but the virtues of burning sulphur must have been well known to Holmes and Watson. Today, joss-sticks are burnt by some for pleasure, but not to cover the smell of bad drains or bugs, though this was considered quite a good ploy a hundred years ago. Holmes and Watson met the 'subtle and aromatic odour' of incense and the 'balsamic odour of the Eastern tobacco' in Thaddeus Sholto's apartment, and were familiar with the smell of shag and ship's tobacco in their own. In their own, too, they were familiar with the smell of firearms discharged at close quarters.

Sherlock Holmes was naturally acquainted with the peculiar odours of a large number of 'chemicals', and even Watson would have recognized sulphuretted hydrogen, carbon disulphide, ether, iodoform and formalin, but neither of them could give a name to the 'thick musky odour' of burning *Radix pedis diaboli*, the secret West African ordeal poison which very nearly did for them. Holmes and Watson had both experienced the smell emitted by opium-pipes and both knew that Lady Frances Carfax's coffin was saturated with chloroform the moment they raised the lid.

Both Holmes and Watson also enjoyed the fragrance of flowers. At least, Holmes did and Watson never seemed to disagree. Holmes maintained that the criminal expert should be able to distinguish seventy-five perfumes and, in *The Hound of the Baskervilles,* he exemplified this by recognizing the scent of white jessamine in Mrs Stapleton's notepaper. He hailed the scent of the rose (in *The Naval Treaty*) as a gratuitous embellishment assuring us of the goodness of Providence, and when he retired to Sussex he rejoiced in the 'thyme-scented Downs'.

He may also have been familiar with the smell of musk (*Mimulus*), a scent which few can remember today because the plant became mysteriously scentless all over the world about 1920. Rumours that the scent of musk has since returned (starting in South America) do not seem to have convinced botanists, though a recovery is presumably possible. The plant is called 'musk' because its scent resembles that of the abdominal gland of the musk-deer, which was the original source of the commercial perfume. Since this odour is due to a ketone called muscone, we may be sure Holmes knew this, too (see page 32).

2
Holmes's Science

WE have to rely chiefly upon Dr Watson for an account of Holmes's scientific knowledge, but, for a man of scientific training, Watson is singularly ignorant of the nature of sciences other than his own. For example, his idea of botany embraces not only the study of 'belladonna, opium and poisons generally', but also 'practical gardening'. Yet he must at least have become acquainted with the nature of botany while reading his elementary biology at medical school. His literary agent should certainly have been able to advise him here, for botany was a compulsory subject in the medical curriculum at Edinburgh University, but, like other literary agents, he probably tended to over-indulgence when reading a profitable client's manuscript.

Holmes probably had a better knowledge of botany than Watson recognized, for he once remarked that 'with a spud, a tin box, and an elementary book on botany, there are instructive days to be spent.' Watson would have done better to have scotched his entry about Holmes's botany and to have put instead: 'Toxicology – excellent practical knowledge.'

Both Holmes and Watson were familiar with the vegetable alkaloids and at their very first meeting Holmes, holding out his hand for inspection, told Watson 'I dabble with poisons a good deal.' Watson noted that his hand was 'all mottled over' with pieces of plaster and discoloured with strong acids. His expertise in pugilism suggests that his hands may have been actually toughened by their acquaintance with the acids, for professional prize-fighters used to pickle theirs in vinegar for this very purpose. However, we should remember that Watson, on the same occasion, says that though 'his hands were invariably blotted with ink and stained with chemicals, yet he was possessed of extraordinary delicacy of touch, as I frequently had occasion to observe when I watched him manipulating his fragile philosophical instruments.' These apparently incongruous characters were possibly exhibited alternately in his violin-playing, for though 'he could play pieces, and difficult pieces', left to himself he would seldom produce any music but 'close his eyes and scrape carelessly at the fiddle which was thrown across his knee.' But then, to soothe Watson's rising discomfort, his fingers would become nimble enough to play 'in quick succession a whole series of my favourite airs.'

According to young Stamford, Holmes was well up in anatomy and we have evidence of this in his recognition of a piece of scorched bone as 'the upper condyle of a human femur'. Those words were actually spoken by Watson, but they were instantly capped by Holmes's 'Exactly!' However, his suggestion in *The Norwood Builder* that the scorched bones of a dog or a couple of rabbits might pass for human remains in the ashes of a fire was undoubtedly ironic. No doubt he found a knowledge of human anatomy of great practical value, but his ignorance of vertebrate zoology suggests that comparative anatomy had no appeal for him.

The shakiness of his zoology was very evident on several occasions. His identification of the 'speckled band' as the non-existent 'swamp-adder' was, to say the least, rash, and (in *The Crooked Man*) he relied on Watson – late of Afghanistan and India – to identify a mongoose for him. Watson was, however, puzzled when Holmes first showed him tracings of the animal's tracks and pointed out that its footmarks had five well-marked footpads,* and said at once, 'It's a dog.' A dog certainly has five pads, one for each of four toes and one for the central 'ball', but a mongoose has five toes all touching the ground and so should leave six pad-marks. However, when Holmes objected that dogs don't run up curtains Watson suggested a monkey instead! Even Holmes knew that monkeys' paws are different, but Watson had no chance of guessing a mongoose until he actually saw the animal.

It would seem that Holmes was scarcely more familiar with the common mole. In *The Boscombe Valley Mystery* he complained of Lestrade's footmarks, saying, 'That left foot of yours with its inward twist is all over the place. A mole could trace it.' He evidently shared the popular but mistaken belief that moles are blind, but his choice of phrase was doubly inappropriate. For one thing, a mole's daily life is spent underground and, for another, the 'blindness' he implies was not that of sight but of understanding. Of course, it was just a hasty remark, but that particular cliché would never have occurred to anybody with a knowledge of moles.

Both Holmes and Watson were more familiar with dogs, the breeds mentioned in the reports of the cases including the bull-pup, bulldog, terrier, Airedale terrier, lurcher, spaniel, beagle, hound, foxhound, wolf-

* He should have said 'pads', of course, or 'foot-pads' with a hyphen. The only dictionary meaning of 'footpad' without a hyphen is a highwayman operating on foot.

hound, Newfoundland, mastiff, and a couple of mongrels (see pages 8–9). The reports also contain references to thirty-five separate species of mammals – not counting the Tiger of San Pedro or the head Llama (*sic*) at Lhasa. But Holmes does not seem to have known very much about any of these creatures beyond what can be gathered from a quick walk round a zoo.

Holmes's serious interest in the invertebrates appears to have been confined to his study of bees during his retirement, and particularly to 'the Segregation of the Queen', though in Watson's reports of his cases he refers to some twelve different species. However, his microscope, always handy, may have tempted him to occasional examinations of the common domestic pests and parasites with which he must have been familiar in his early London period. These would have included flies, ants, clothes moths, mosquitoes, crickets, cockroaches, wasps, blackbeetles, spiders, earwigs, woodlice, fleas, bugs, mites, ticks, lice, weevils, firebrats and silverfish. His notes include a reference to a poisonous worm and possibly other horrors but, except for that deadly Medusa, *Cyanea Capillata* (the 'Lion's Mane'), which he read up in J. G. Wood's *Out of Doors*, these were generally unknown to science and not available for study. The remarkably large number of names of animals (adults and young) mentioned in the stories gives an exaggerated idea of Holmes's knowledge of zoology, but the curious will find them listed in the Appendix.

Watson does not mention Holmes's practical, if limited, knowledge of pathology, yet Stamford describes one of his early experiments as 'beating the subjects in the dissecting-rooms with a stick . . . to verify how far bruises may be produced after death.' Holmes discovered the force required to drive a harpoon through a human body by practising on a pig's carcass, and his *sang froid* was such that (in *The Resident Patient*) he could examine the dead body of a man hanging from the ceiling by a rope so that his neck 'was drawn out like a plucked chicken's', and give a short exposition of his methods of detection before bothering to cut him down. He was sufficiently knowledgeable on the symptoms of a disease of the coolies in Sumatra to be able to deceive the world's greatest authority on the subject by pretending to be suffering from it, and he was familiar with Tapanuli fever and the black Formosa corruption – both totally unknown to Dr Watson.

Stamford also told Watson that Holmes was a 'first-class chemist. . . . His studies are very desultory and eccentric, but he has amassed a lot of out-of-the-way knowledge which would astonish his professors.' At medical school Watson would also have studied chemistry to rather less than matriculation standard, but advanced chemistry would not have appeared anywhere in the medical curriculum, so that when he judges Holmes's knowledge of chemistry to be 'profound' he may only mean far beyond his own knowledge of the subject. It was, in fact, some way into organic chemistry, yet both Watson and Holmes failed to come up to the mark in explaining the luminosity of the hound of the Baskervilles, though here Holmes may simply have been reticent in the presence of the shocked Sir Henry.

When the hound is killed, Watson noted that 'the huge jaws seemed to be dripping with a bluish flame'. He then placed his hand upon the glowing muzzle and held up his fingers, which 'smouldered and gleamed in the darkness.' Without further investigation he announces that it is phosphorus, but this is probably because he did not know of any other phosphorescent substance. He should, however, have known that yellow phosphorus – the kind which glows – has a strong garlic-like odour. Holmes recognizes this because he immediately adds, 'A cunning preparation of it. There is no smell which might have interfered with his power of scent.' This remark is, of course ironic, for Holmes must have known that it would not be possible to eliminate the smell of the phosphorus if it were still exposed to the air, and this was necessary for its luminosity.*

Further, his knowledge of toxicology would have told him that had the hound been daubed with yellow phosphorus in that way, even on only one occasion, it would almost certainly have been fatally poisoned. Four grains ingested with the saliva would probably have killed it within twelve hours, and certainly within two days, and meanwhile it would have been rolling on the ground in agony. Watson, as a doctor, might be expected to have known this, too! But Holmes's more profound knowledge of chemistry would instantly have brought to his mind at least three other phosphorescent substances which could have been safely used instead of phosphorus.

These are calcium sulphide, zinc sulphide, and barium sulphide ('sulphide of baryta'), all of which become phosphorescent if they contain metallic im-

* Holmes was sometimes given to this sort of leg-pulling irony, another well-known instance being his remark when Inspector Lestrade asked him (in *The Norwood Builder*), 'You are aware that no two thumb-marks are alike?' That Holmes's dry rejoinder, 'I have heard something of the kind,' was ironic has been pointed out by Martin Dakin in *A Sherlock Holmes Commentary*, for Holmes was undoubtedly familiar with the significance of finger-prints at that time.

purities and are exposed to light for a short while. When the light is removed they will continue to shine for a much longer time, though probably not very brightly after four hours. On an October evening there is very little daylight after six o'clock and Sir Henry Baskerville did not leave the Stapleton's until about twenty past ten, so that the phosphor was probably excited by a lamp for some time before it was actually wanted. But this could easily have been arranged in a screened corner of the miner's cottage where the hound was kept, though the substance would have had to be put into a glass jar or a wide shallow dish to get maximum benefit from the light. The 'tin' that was found was doubtless where the sulphide was stored when not being used. These phosphors have no noticeable scent, are not poisonous in small quantities, and are commonly used in luminous paint.* Stapleton would probably have chosen zinc sulphide if it was obtainable without difficulty, but he could have made calcium sulphide himself from lime and sulphur, adding the necessary impurities. It is a pity Holmes did not take some home for analysis – a metallic sulphide would have been right up his street.

One of his successful efforts at analysis (in *A Case of Identity*) was to determine 'bisulphate of baryta', probably the salt now known as barium peroxodisulphate (in America, peroxydisulfate), $BaS_2O_8.H_2O$. But this was simple. For any senior schoolboy it would have been mere routine in the practical chemistry class. However, in the more advanced field of organic chemistry we find Holmes engaged in the 'classification of the acetones'.

* In modern times a trace of a radioactive substance is added to zinc sulphide to make the glow permanent and suitable for use in watches, clocks, compasses, etc.

At least, that is what he said, but since acetone is merely the simplest of the ketones, it was undoubtedly the ketones that he was classifying.

In *The Sign of Four,* we read that Holmes 'busied himself all the evening in an abstruse chemical analysis which involved much heating of retorts and distilling of vapours, ending at last in a smell which fairly drove me out of the apartment. Up to the small hours of the morning I could hear the clinking of his test-tubes, which told me that he was still engaged in his malodorous experiment.' And in *The Naval Treaty* Watson finds Holmes in his dressing-gown boiling something in a retort over a Bunsen burner, and condensing the distillate in a two-litre measure. He then did some quick work with a pipette, dipping it into 'this bottle or that', and finally testing the result with litmus paper. 'If this paper remains blue, all is well. If it turns red, it means a man's life.' It turned a 'dull, dirty crimson', so we assume that somebody went to the gallows.

This, of course, has nothing to do with his famous precipitation test for haemoglobin, which he first demonstrated to Watson in 1881, on the day they met at Barts. He never disclosed the secret of this test, but pathologists are no longer interested because chemical tests have now been largely superseded by spectroscopic examination. Chemistry was not only employed by Holmes in his detective work; it was also a hobby and means of relaxation. In *The Sign of Four,* for example, he says 'I gave my mind a thorough rest by plunging into chemical analysis,' and he doubtless contributed many new items of chemical knowledge to the science, though they were either reported anonymously or he never bothered to disclose them.

At Montpellier, in 1894, he 'spent some months in

a research into the coal-tar derivatives' which, in those days, would have meant the aromatic carbon compounds, such as benzene, naphthalene, anthracene, phenol, toluol, pyridine and aniline. Holmes may have been interested in aniline dyes, or perhaps he was on the track of aspirin, which was prepared from phenol by the German firm of Bayer in 1899, but he was not – as some writers have suggested – working on plastics. Except for celluloid (or xylonite), plastics were quite unknown until 1897, when a cat accidentally invented casein plastics by upsetting a beaker of formaldehyde on to some cheese.

At Montepellier, Holmes undoubtedly had the use of a properly equipped laboratory, but if it is ever doubted that chemistry of the Baker Street kind could be satisfactorily conducted on a small table in the corner of a sitting-room, it should be remembered that William Hyde Wollaston, FRS, the discover of the elements palladium, rhodium, niobium, and titanium, had even less equipment. When a distinguished foreign scientist called on him with a letter of introduction and asked to see his laboratory, Wollaston willingly obliged and 'immediately produced a small tray containing some glass tubes, a simple blow-pipe or bent metal tube, worth a few pence only, two or three common watch-glasses, a slip of platinum, and a few similar things.'* These last included a tailor's thimble, used as a galvanic battery. Holmes was very much better provided for than this and is, indeed, not known to have complained of lack of chemical facilities.

However, we need not suppose that there was a

* Dr John Ayrton Paris, quoted by Ralf and Chandos Temple in *Invention and Discovery*, Groombridge and Sons, Paternoster Row, *c.* 1870.

water-tap in the sitting-room at 221B, for Holmes, as an analyst, would certainly have kept a large vessel of distilled water fitted with a ground-glass tap for easy use when measuring quantities. It was probably on a bracket in the corner of the room. Under his work table he probably kept a two or three gallon tank for waste liquids. It would have been made of glass or pottery, for the acids he constantly used would have attacked a metal bucket or an enamel slop-pail. Also, the bathroom must have been quite handy, both for emptying the waste-tank and getting occasional tap-water, for there are some purposes for which it would be gross extravagance to use the distilled.

A brief glance of him at work was given in the original text of *The Resident Patient,* as printed in *The Strand* magazine for August, 1893. The passage is omitted from all later reprints but Martin Dakin quotes it in full in his *A Sherlock Holmes Commentary.* The relevant sentences state that Holmes 'was deep in some of those abstruse chemical investigations which absorbed him utterly as long as he was engaged upon them. Towards evening, however, the breaking of a test-tube brought his research to a premature ending, and he sprang up from his chair with an exclamation of impatience and a clouded brow. "A day's work ruined, Watson", said he, striding across to the window.'

Both Holmes and Watson seem to have taken a brooding sort of interest in archaeology, and particularly in the Stone Age relics of Dartmoor and Cornwall. Holmes even resided for some time in an old stone hut on Dartmoor, but this was in Sir Henry Baskerville's interest, not to study archaeology. However, in 1894, Holmes was involved in a case tantalizingly referred to by Watson (in *The Golden Pince-nez*) as 'the Addleton tragedy and the singular contents of the ancient British barrow,' and this may have aroused a genuine interest in the subject.

In describing the scene of *The Devil's Foot* tragedy, Watson wrote that in

> every direction upon the moors there were traces of some vanished race which had passed utterly away, and left as its sole record strange monuments of stone, irregular mounds which contained the burned ashes of the dead, and curious earthworks which hinted at prehistoric strife. The glamour and mystery of the place, with its sinister atmosphere . . . appealed to the imagination of my friend. . . . The vicar of the parish, Mr Roundhay, was something of an archaeologist, and as such Holmes had made his acquaintance.

The walk along the Cornish cliffs described in the same story affords evidence that Holmes had already acquired some local knowledge and knew the limitations of the region for collectable items, though Watson failed to appreciate the irony of his proposal, 'Let us walk along the cliffs together and search for flint arrows.' Nothing could be less likely than that they should find a flint arrowhead on the Devonian rocks skirting Poldhu Bay and Holmes was merely giving vent to another ironic 'Sherlockism' of the type exemplified on page 30. That is, knowing there were no arrows to be found, he made his cryptic remark as a neat way of saying, 'It is hopeless to try to find any clues to the mystery today, so we might as well go for a walk and look for arrows, for all the good it will do us.' In fact, he adds, 'We are more likely to find them than clues to this problem,' thus emphasizing the hopelessness of the task. Watson then tells how they 'skirted the cliffs' wrestling with their problem but with no further mention of arrows, though an hour or so later they did decide to 'devote the rest of our morning to the pursuit of neolithic man.'

Sherlock Holmes's knowledge of astronomy, according to Dr Watson when they first met in 1881, was nil. 'He was ignorant of the Copernican Theory and of the composition of the Solar System.' When Watson informed him that the earth travelled round the sun Holmes said, 'Now that I do know it I shall do my best to forget it.' Nevertheless, it must have stuck in his mind and eventually goaded him to look it up, probably in his encyclopaedia, for in 1888 he was discussing with Watson the causes of the change in the obliquity of the ecliptic. One doubts if this discussion could have led anywhere and Holmes probably gave the whole subject up after a glance at Professor Moriarty's advanced treatise on *The Dynamics of an Asteroid.*

Watson states that Holmes's knowledge of geology was 'practical but limited' and, by way of example, notes that Holmes 'has shown me splashes upon his trousers, and told me by their colour and consistence in what part of London he had received them.' This is evidently Watson's idea of geology but, however that may be, Holmes could certainly distinguish several different types of soil by their physical appearance and describe them in what Watson would no doubt regard as geological terms. These include stone, rock, pebble, shingle, gravel, sand, mud, clay, mire, ooze, earth, mould and chalk.

In one famous passage Holmes deduces that Watson has been to the Wigmore Street Post Office from 'a little reddish mould adhering to your instep', for 'they have taken up the pavement and thrown up some earth . . . of this peculiar reddish tint which is found, as far as I know, nowhere else in the neighbourhood.' But so much of the material used for making up London's roads came from distant quarries and gravel-pits that a geological map based on Holmes's data would have been absolutely worthless – as a geological map. But as a map of the surface activities of the Metropolitan Board of Works it might have had value in many directions besides that of tracing criminals.

However, if this was not geology Holmes did have some knowledge of both petrology and mineralogy, which are generally regarded as two of the branches of geology. We may conclude that Watson had far too few opportunities to display Holmes's familiarity with these subjects, though chalk, flint, clay and the granite of Dartmoor are all referred to. We find also that Holmes is able to recognize (generally on sight) the minerals amethyst, beryl, diamond, emerald, ruby and sapphire. The mazarin ('dark blue') stone was probably a sapphire, and the blue carbuncle a variety of cyprine (blue vesuvianite) cut *en cabochon.*

Holmes also made at least two essays in descriptive geology, one remarkable for being completely wrong and the other for being completely right. However, it is only fair to point out that while he was seldom in the wrongly described neighbourhood, he had spent about six years of almost daily observation in the other, correctly describing it on the spot. Both are concerned with chalk, a substance about the uses of which Watson seems to have had some strange ideas. According to Holmes, Watson put billiard chalk on his fingers 'to steady the cue', though for this purpose he would have done better to have used French chalk (talc). And Watson himself observed that Lord Mount-James was so full of gout that he could have chalked his billiard cue with his knuckles, but failed to suggest that he might have steadied his cue by resting it on his knuckles instead of the usual part of the fingers. Of course, none of these substances is chalk, in the geological sense, but it would be unfair to expect Watson to know that.

But this is a digression and Holmes's two geological essays have still to be described. To take first the one which was completely wrong, John Openshaw, who consulted Holmes about 1887 on the matter of *The Five Orange Pips,* was perceived by Holmes to 'have come up from the south-west.' 'Yes, from Horsham,' admits Openshaw. Then Holmes says, 'That clay and chalk mixture which I see upon your toe-caps is quite distinctive.'

Now, a clay and chalk mixture could be a description of the Lower Chalk formation, or of a marly band in the Middle Chalk, but not of anything nearer to Horsham than Dorking, eleven and a half miles to the north. Horsham stands on the sands and clays of the Hastings Beds, near the centre of a vast area of the Weald Clay. Surrounding this are a belt of Lower Greensand and a strip of Gault clay before any chalk is reached. The South Downs are as far to the south as Box Hill is to the north, so Openshaw could not have stubbed his toe in the chalk in that direction either. (*See* fig. 1.)

He would have certainly have taken the train to London from Horsham, his nearest station, so that he could not have got chalk on his boots unless he had alighted at an intermediate stop and gone for a cross-country ramble in the rain. This is not in the least plausible, even as an explanation of his arrival so late in the evening. Yet Holmes undoubtedly spotted something which looked like clay mixed with chalk on Openshaw's toe-caps; but if it was not this, what was it? Modelling clay or pipe-clay would have washed off instantly in the heavy rain, and so would lime or white-

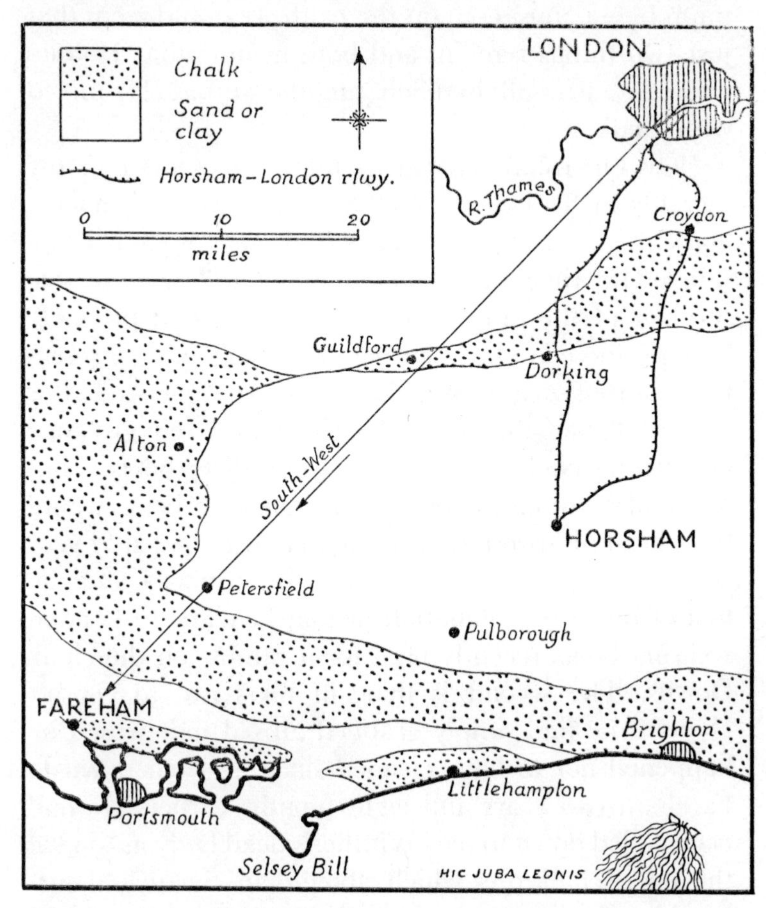

Fig. 1. A simplified map showing that Horsham is about as far away from any chalk as it is possible to get in this part of the country. So, did the chalk on John Openshaw's boots come from Fareham? See the text.

wash. William Cobbett once compared the sticky clayey-chalk mixture to 'grey soap', but Openshaw is no more likely to have had grey soap on his toe-caps than baker's dough. We may surely rule out these substances as impossible in the circumstances, but then, as Holmes frequently remarked, what remains, however improbable, must contain the truth. It would seem that just two things remain, and both assume that Holmes was right, after all, in diagnosing the stuff as clay mixed with chalk.

Now, Openshaw's narrative makes no mention of any servants in his household, though his deceased uncle's housemaid, Mary, may have continued with his late father and then stayed to serve young John, the sole survivor of the family. If this is so, she had probably been promoted to housekeeper or cook-general, or something of that sort, for somebody had clearly looked after him well enough. He is described as 'well groomed and trimly clad' – except for those dirty boots – but Mary already had enough to do and the boots would have been his own responsibility. He was evidently very lax in the matter of cleaning them regularly and the first of the two explanations is that he came to London wearing boots recently used for a ramble on the chalk Downs. The second is that, in his haste to consult Holmes, he had simply grabbed an old pair which he happened not to have cleaned since he went down to Fareham two years and eight months earlier. He had been called down to see his father's dead body in 'one of the deep chalk-pits which abound in the neighbourhood,' and when he got home he was evidently so overcome by grief that he shoved his dirty boots away into some corner. There they remained, uncleaned, until they were fished out by chance in the haste of catching the train to London. There was, of course, no time to clean off the mixture of clay and chalk from the toecaps. If we have to choose between these two theories we should not forget that, while we have no evidence that Openshaw went for a ramble, we do know for certain that he was in a chalk-pit near Fareham.*

Holmes's absolutely correct (though not very detailed) geological description refers to the coast at his Sussex retreat. He gives a very good account of the cliffs of marly Lower Chalk and, beneath them, the reefs of Upper Greensand which hold pools at low tide. He refers to 'small grottos and caves in the base of the cliffs', but in fact the chalk coast of Sussex shows only the characteristic 'nick' at the foot of the cliffs where they are more or less vertical.* An extra deep hollow in the nick might seem like a cave or grotto to someone taking shelter in it, and Holmes may have done just this on occasion. He also says that the shingle beach was broken at one point, 'where the little cove and village of Fulworth break the line.' By 'cove' he may have meant simply 'hollow' or 'valley', though another possible meaning is given below, but this coast never boasted a cove in the west-country sense of a small deep bay. If the line of the beach was 'broken' it was probably because, for one short stretch only, the shingle was scarcely deep enough to cover the reef-rocks and had been cleared to provide a clean path down to the sea.

At this point, then, lay the village of Fulworth and, a little inland, on a slope of the Downs, stood what

* This would also make Holmes literally correct in deducing that Openshaw came from the south-west, for Fareham is *exactly* south-west of London whereas Horsham is almost due south. True, it was not Holmes who mentioned Horsham, but the weakness of his geology is shown by his tacit acceptance of it as the place of origin of the chalk.

* Two or three small artificial caves for the shelter of shipwrecked seamen have been dug out beneath the old Belle Toute lighthouse, midway between Birling Gap and Beachy Head, but, except for 'Parson Darby's Hole', they were not there in Holmes's time and in any case the spot is too remote to be safely visited between tides.

Holmes called his 'villa'. He describes his slope of the Downs as 'southern', but no truly southern slope breaks the cliffs anywhere along this coast. The slopes fall away roughly to the south-east, but with enough irregularities of dry valley and coomb to provide many a south-facing site, which is all he needed to command 'a great view of the Channel'.

So where is Fulworth? Holmes's excellent geology leaves little room for doubt and rules the oft-cited Birling Gap and Cuckmere Haven right out of court. They may be dismissed because the cliffs at both places are in the Upper Chalk, there are no rocks on or under the beach to provide bathing-pools, and neither place boasted a police station.* But *all* these requirements are met on the coast immediately to the east of Beachy Head, and when Holmes first settled there the area was as wild and deserted as he implies. (*See* fig. 2.) It was still pretty well isolated as late as the 1920s and even today the area has been carefully preserved as a beauty spot, though it falls within the modern boundaries of Eastbourne. To appreciate what it was like when Holmes settled there we have only to review the recent history of Eastbourne.

In the early nineteenth century there were only four hamlets in the area now covered by the town: East Bourne, a mile and a half inland; South Bourne, the region between the present railway station and the pier; Sea Houses, a fishing village at the Redoubt; and Meads, a tiny hamlet separated from the others by open country. In the ordnance map of 1893 South Bourne and Sea Houses had grown together to make what was known as the New Town, and they were con-

* The rocks marked at Birling Gap in the *AA Book of the Seaside* (1972) are a mistake.

nected by few roads with fewer houses to East Bourne, then – as now – called the Old Town. Meads was still pretty well cut off and contained only three or four short narrow roads, with a roundabout route to Old

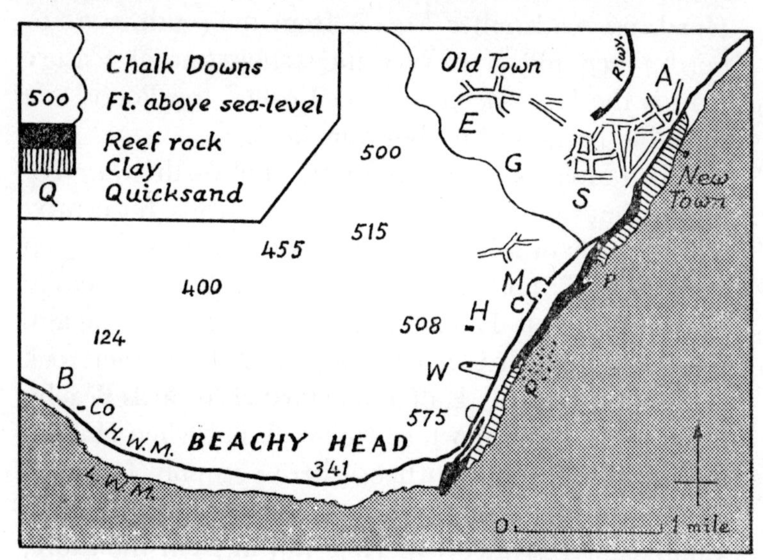

Fig. 2. The original four hamlets comprising Eastbourne: E (East Bourne), S (South Bourne), M (Meads) and A (Sea Houses). G, Golf links permanently separating East Bourne ('Old Town') from Meads. H, Holywell House. W, Whitebread Hole. B, Birling Gap. *H.W.M.*, High water mark. *L.W.M.*, Low water mark. *c*, Old chalk-pit, now gardens. *p*, The Pound. *Co*, Coastguard. Except where the reefs occur the shores are covered with flint shingle. *Note*: The (fictitious) 'roads' betoken built-up areas.

Town and a coast road not yet built up to New Town. It was virtually surrounded by country open enough for laying out the large golf course which still separates it from Old Town.

The four hamlets were united to form the borough of Eastbourne as early as 1883, but Meads remained a country hamlet to all intents and purposes. It did not become plainly an outlying part of the town until about 1910, and then only by virtue of the building of a few large private houses standing in their own grounds along the coastal road. Apart from the road to Beachy Head, no roads enter Meads from the south, west or north, even today. A very interesting coastal feature here is the large deep rock-pool called the Pound – a veritable paradise for 'lion's manes'!

When Holmes settled in Sussex 'Fulworth' was very likely what survived of the hamlet of Meads, for nearby was the relic of a large old chalk quarry, running deep into the cliffs and open to the shore. It might easily have appealed to Holmes as a 'cove'* and here, again, the shingle beach is bordered by reefs of harder rock (Upper Greensand). Half a mile farther towards Beachy Head is the area known as Holywell, but when Holmes settled in the neighbourhood there was only Holywell House. A little farther still, to the south-west, a narrow valley called Whitebread Hole ran in from the shore, but seawards of the shingle here was a patch of quicksand – not a place for bathing. Holmes's 'villa' could have been the building, facing south, at the head of Whitebread Hole, and Holywell House could well have been 'The Gables', Harold Stackhurst's coaching establishment.

In brief, this short stretch of coast contains, at various spots not a quarter of a mile apart, all the features Holmes refers to, and if Dr Watson's agent ever took a stroll from Eastbourne along the modern coastal walks, he must have instantly recognized them from the de-

* It has now been half filled in and made into a sheltered retreat with lawns, rockeries, pergolas, etc, and is fronted by a row of bathing huts. Though named 'Holywell Gardens' it is half a mile from Holywell House.

scriptions in his client's manuscripts. For the greater part of the year this was still a pretty deserted stretch of coast, even in the 1940s, ending in a hard climb straight up to the top of Beachy Head. The general location of ' Fulworth ' is thus satisfactorily established by Holmes's own excellent account of the geology and natural features of the district, though we cannot pinpoint the village unless it was Meads.

So much we owe to his geology, then. There remains but one science to consider – his own special science of Detection. The title of his *magnum opus* was to be *The Whole Art of Detection*, for it is surely an art no less than a science and a technology. In fact, it deserves a new name, and what could be more appropriate for a skill based on subtle observation, a detailed and accurate memory, and native cunning, than *metagrabology* (μεταγραβολογία), a word cognate with Rabelais's *metagraboulizer*? The English version of this, according to the Oxford Dictionary, is 'metagrobolize', to puzzle or puzzle out, and if Holmes is to be awarded a posthumous degree it should surely match Watson's with another MD – Doctor of Metagrabology.

But he was also a Master of Zetetics, the art of enquiry (from the Greek ζητητικός), and this bears the same important relation to metagrabology that gardening does to botany. To give but one example of Holmes's skill in this field, we cannot but admire – or can we? – his method of extracting from the servant Bannister the information which betrayed young Gilchrist, the guilty one of the Three Students. Bannister had loyally and stubbornly refused to give away the son of his old employer, so Holmes sent for Gilchrist and, in front of Bannister, demanded to know 'how you, an honourable man, ever came to commit such an action as that of yesterday?' Gilchrist cast a look of horror and reproach at Bannister, who cried out, 'No, no, Mr Gilchrist, sir; I never said a word – never one word!' 'No, but you have now,' said Holmes.

There is doubtless a whole section on methods of obtaining information from reluctant witnesses without employing the crudities of a Gestapo in Holmes's text book. That this work was never published can only be regarded as a national misfortune, but it is possible that the chapters consisting of reprinted monographs are all that ever existed except in the form of notes. Should further manuscripts come to light, however, we can surely hope that at least a volume of collectanea will see print.

We reproduce in figure 3 the title-page we should like to have seen in the 1940s, but the Second World War intervened and the government failed to provide a grant for the establishment of a university at Fulworth. Had they done so, the long-awaited masterpiece (fully illustrated by young Mycroft Sherrinford-Vernet) would surely have appeared – to take pride of place in the police libraries of the world.

THE WHOLE ART
OF
DETECTION

BY

SHERLOCK HOLMES, M.D., M.Z.

Watsonian Professor of Metagrabology and
the Zetetic Sciences, Meads College,
the University of Fulworth

ILLUSTRATED BY
M. SHERRINFORD-VERNET

THE FULWORTH PRESS

Fig. 3. A proposed title-page for Holmes's great unpublished treatise, printed in Baskerville type.

3
The Monographs

WE know little of Sherlock Holmes's writings beyond their titles or subjects, but our knowledge of his methods and principles enables us to make shrewd guesses at some of their contents. For example, in 1887 Holmes proposed to write 'another little monograph' *Upon the Typewriter and its Relation to Crime.* There is not the slightest doubt that this work – if it ever materialized – showed how an individual typewriter could be identified by such accidental characteristics as blemished, misaligned, or unevenly worn letters. In *A Case of Identity* he gives examples from fourteen distinguishing features which he had noted in a letter typed by Mr Windibank, and he might well have cited these by way of illustration. But we can safely assume that his paper would cover a much wider field than this.

In *The Hound of the Baskervilles* Holmes declares that 'the detection of types is one of the most elementary branches of knowledge to the special expert in crime.' It is true that he is referring to the types used for printing newspapers, which he describes as his 'special hobby', but it is unlikely that he would have neglected those used in typewriters, at any rate from about 1886, when they first began to be widely used.

He recognized 'the leaded bourgeois type of a *Times* article' instantly, and we can hardly doubt that he would know a *Yöst* typescript the moment he saw it. When he was very young, he tells us, he once 'confused the *Leeds Mercury* with the *Western Morning News*', and it would not necessarily imply a lack of interest in typewriters if he once – or even twice – confused a *Remington* with a *Bar-Lock.*

Typewriters were not very common when Holmes solved Mary Sutherland's problem, nor were they very efficient. Miss Sutherland considered she was doing 'pretty well' typing 'from fifteen to twenty sheets in a day.' Probably much fiddling, adjusting and re-typing was necessary, for three or four hours would have sufficed on a modern machine, even for a two-fingered amateur. Mr Windibank probably used the much extolled *Hammond Ideal* (1884), for the *Yöst* had not yet appeared in Europe and a satisfactory *Remington* (the successor to *Sholes and Glidden,* 1876) did not appear until 1888. It does not seem very likely that Holmes wrote his monograph until the very end of the century when there was a much larger variety of models available, though many of them retained such primitive devices as inking by carbon paper (*Daw and Tait,* 1884; *Hardy,* 1895) and inking by a pad (*Maskelyne,* 1889; *Victor,* 1894). In some machines inking was done by means of a roller (*Cox,* 1870), and in others by an inked textile sheet (*Hall,* 1881) or a hand-fed ribbon. The first satisfactory automatically-fed ribbon was *Remington's* of 1896.

All these different devices would have left distinguishing marks, and so would the multifarious mechanisms employed. In the *Hammond* machine, for instance, a hammer hit the paper on to the type, which was mounted on a pair of 'swinging sectors'. In the *Columbia* (1886) the type was carried on the rim of a wheel, in the *Blickensderfer* (1893) on a drum, and in the *Crandall* (1893) on a 'sleeve'. The *Lambert* (1896) employed a 'radial striking plunger', while the *Maskelyne* (1889) had a 'grasshopper' mechanism.

Machines with the type mounted on levers (as in most modern typewriters) were variously described as 'radial striking type-bar' (*Ford*, 1896), 'up-stroke type-bar' (*Remington No. 1*, 1876), 'down-stroke type-bar from front' (*Bar-Lock*, 1889), ditto 'from sides' (*Oliver*, 1894), and ditto 'from rear' (*Fitch*, 1886). All these mechanisms – and many more – left impresses which must have differed in minute details, but Holmes would have shown how to spot them with a magnifying glass and no doubt listed them all in his monograph.

The blackness or faintness of the type would have told him at once the degree to which a ribbon had been used and at what point a new ribbon had been inserted, while the microscope would show the characteristic texture of the ribbon used. Holmes's study of the coal-tar derivatives at Montpellier in 1894 (see page 33) would probably have enabled him to distinguish the aniline compounds used in typewriting inks. He would certainly not have neglected this aspect of typewriter detection, for the use of different colours was introduced in the 1890s and the *Smith Premier* of 1895 even had a *three*-colour ribbon.

Further, he would undoubtedly have evolved a system of clues to the physical and even mental characteristics of the typist. In 1895 he very nearly made the mistake of assuming that Miss Violet Smith, the 'Solitary Cyclist', was a typist from her spatulate finger-tips, but decided against it because of the 'spirituality about the face'. This was too unlikely in a typist though natural enough in a pianist. A typist may also be identified by an examination of her sleeves, as Holmes demonstrated in *A Case of Identity*:

As you observe, this woman [Miss Mary Sutherland] had plush on her sleeves, which is a most useful material for showing traces. The double line a little above the wrist, where the typewritist presses against the table, was beautifully defined. The sewing-machine, of the hand type, leaves a similar mark, but only on the left arm, and on the side of it farthest from the thumb, instead of being right across the broadest part, as this was.

Further, one would have thought that such sleeve-marks on a typist might indicate a very lackadaisical and irresponsible character, or else that she was on the point of collapse. It is almost impossible to type properly with one's wrists resting on the edge of the table, and a typist with any regard at all for the quality of her work would not continue if she were that tired.

Many other clues to the physical condition of a typist may be found. For example, since T comes in the bank above F and G on a standard keyboard, a typist who persistently strikes the T when she should put F or G probably has long finger-nails. Uneven impresses would indicate the amateur, full-stops that have punched holes through the paper a heavy-handed two-finger performer, and blotted o's, e's, a's and m's a slovenly and lazy character – or, alternatively, a poor friendless person who could neither buy nor borrow a pin and was using a machine belonging to a slovenly and lazy character.

Frequent erasures might be accounted for in many ways. The typist might be a bad speller, a foreigner who neglected to refer to his dictionary soon enough, a person suffering from the 'hte-for-the' complex, from poor sight, or even from a large family living in one room. A page of typescript with a reversed carbon copy on the back would suggest gross carelessness in several directions, while letters which are half red and half black could be a dead give-away, even to Watson. Holmes would doubtless have covered all these points so thoroughly that a student of his monograph would be able to put his finger instantly on one of a hundred typists in a large block of offices and identify her as the writer of some particular letter (in either sense of the word).

It was not until 1903 that Holmes remarked 'I have serious thoughts of writing a small monograph' *Upon the Uses of Dogs in the Work of the Detective.* It is rather surprising that he had not written on this subject before, because he had certainly made use of dogs on several earlier occasions. Even as far back as 1881, in *A Study in Scarlet,* he had found an excellent use for old and decrepit terriers: to test the poisonous properties of pills of unknown composition. The method was simplicity itself:

> With a perfect shriek of delight he rushed to the box, cut the other pill in two, dissolved it, added milk, and presented it to the terrier. The unfortunate creature's tongue seemed hardly to have been moistened in it before it gave a convulsive shiver in every limb, and lay as rigid and lifeless as if it had been struck by lightning.
>
> Sherlock Holmes drew a long breath, and wiped the perspiration from his forehead.

He must have been very much out of condition, one would think, to perspire so after only one shriek and cutting only one pill with a knife, but even before the shriek, Watson tells us, he was 'springing from his chair and pacing wildly up and down the room.' And no doubt it was a close, muggy day.

But valuable as this use of old dogs might be in some countries, in England it must take a very minor place before tracking, pointing, guarding, warning, guiding, identifying, man-handling, and killing, many of which functions were exemplified in Watson's reports of Holmes's cases. Holmes expressed his faith in dogs at Shoscombe Old Place when he said, 'Dogs don't make mistakes,' a remark made all the more forceful by coming immediately after Holmes had seen it make one. 'He thought it was his mistress and he found it was a stranger' – a clear enough mistake, one would have thought! However, the upshot was that the spaniel identified the passenger in the carriage as a man in disguise, and Holmes would not be likely to omit a reference to it in his monograph.

When Holmes told the Shoscombe inn-keeper 'I am a dog-fancier myself,' we may take this as merely a part of his conversational tactics in probing for information, for he does not seem to have been very knowledgeable about dogs, or to have been particularly fond of them. Watson's bull-pup did not stay very long with him in Baker Street and, since Mrs Hudson kept a dog herself, we can only suppose that it was Holmes who had raised objections. After all, it was Victor Trevor's bull-terrier which had seized his ankle when he was at college and laid him by the heels for ten days, as he mentions in the case of *The 'Gloria Scott'*.

Holmes's interest in dogs was obviously confined to their use by the criminal expert, though his monograph would certainly have included an illustrated section on the identification of dogs by their tooth-marks. He displayed his familiarity with this subject when he deduced that Dr Mortimer's dog was a curly-haired spaniel from the marks on his walking-stick. Another paragraph would surely deal with the sympathetic relations between a dog and the people who owned it.

'Whoever saw a frisky dog in a gloomy family?' he asks (in *The Creeping Man*), 'or a sad dog in a happy one? Snarling people have snarling dogs, dangerous people have dangerous ones. And their passing moods may reflect the passing moods of others.' Watson regarded this as far-fetched, but Holmes thought it offered a way of finding out why Professor Presbury's faithful wolfhound, Roy, endeavoured to bite him. And when it finally succeeded in sinking its fangs deep into the Professor's throat, 'Bennett's voice and presence brought the great hound instantly to reason' – a further example of sympathy between canine and human moods.

Neither Watson nor Holmes hesitated to shoot other people's dangerous dogs when they were a risk to human life. Holmes dispatched the Hound of the Baskervilles with five rapid revolver shots, and Watson blew the brains out of Mr Rucastle's mastiff with one shot from his service revolver. However, the monograph would not be likely to dwell on the shooting of dogs, though it would certainly explain how to pacify or silence guard dogs. When Holmes applied to Dr Armstrong's coachman for information about the *Missing Three-quarter,* 'he was rude enough to set a dog at me. Neither dog nor man liked the look of my stick, however.' But there would be more to it than that and the behaviour of guard dogs would merit the most detailed treatment. No doubt there would be a reference to the case of *Silver Blaize* and the curious incident of the dog in the night-time. The 'curious incident' was, of course, that the dog did nothing in the night-time.

Holmes was certainly familiar with the use of dogs for tracking. We have already given examples of this (pages 8–9) and noted his preference for mongrels. Had Holmes been practising at the present day, his monograph would doubtless have included full instructions for training dogs to sniff out drugs and explosives. Modern police dogs are chiefly Alsatians and Labradors, but Holmes does not seem to have favoured either breed, nor the bloodhounds or 'sleuth-hounds' recommended by Watson in *The Creeping Man.* His neglect of the bloodhound was later used to throw doubt on his detective skill by publisher Alfred Harmsworth. Ever since 1894, Harmsworth had been mocking him by printing alleged reports of the preposterous activities of a fictitious Baker Street detective called Sexton Blake, a matter which calls for a slight digression.

What Holmes had found out to provoke Harmsworth's antagonism is unknown, but there seems little doubt that he was aiming either to ruin Holmes's reputation or, in some way, to cash in on it. His fictitious reports certainly achieved enormous sales. By the end of the century Holmes had already become a legend, and nothing is easier to gate-crash than a legend. It does not matter who King Arthur was, or if he ever lived at all, it will always be possible to make money out of him. Similarly, it no longer seemed to matter who the great 'Baker Street detective' was, so long as everybody believed there was an address in Baker Street to go to. And Harmsworth took pains to make Sexton Blake appear a more normal, reliable human being than Holmes looked in the published pictures of him. Instead of sporting a theatrical deerstalker and inverness cape, and smoking a calabash pipe, Sexton Blake wore a common bowler hat and was described as a well-built

Victorian gentleman, and he carried nothing more exotic than a heavy stick. Obviously he was the real detective and Holmes the phoney.

When Holmes retired to Sussex to keep bees in 1903, and was no longer available to people who still sought his help, Harmsworth continued to misdirect would-be clients to the non-existent Blake. When it was at last realized that there was *no* Blake, certain lewd fellows of the baser sort began to spread the rumour that perhaps there was no Holmes, either! Holmes's clients and their friends knew better, of course, but Scotland Yard thought it good for Lestrade's and Gregson's reputations to let the thing ride.

Further, the 'information' Harmsworth put out about Sexton Blake was sometimes, and in some respects, similar to that related of Sherlock Holmes but reduced to absurdity. For example, after Holmes had retired to Sussex, Blake was alleged to have retired to the country as 'Henry Park'. But when Henry Park was accused of a local robbery, Sexton Blake promptly turned up again in Baker Street and was engaged to track himself down! Holmes may then have recollected how, in Baker Street also, he had been asked by Lestrade to track down himself and Watson for the murder of Charles Augustus Milverton in 1899. What a mockery! And it was immediately after this, in 1904, that the 'superiority' of the fictitious Blake was clumsily suggested by his spectacular use of a bloodhound named Pedro. This somewhat belated dig at Holmes suggested that his neglect of this celebrated breed implied either ignorance or incompetence. One can imagine Holmes's comments to Watson on the long-distance telephone:

Wonders will never cease, Watson! There seem to be no limits to the credulity of the great British public. That man Harmsworth has added a phantom bloodhound to his phantom detective, but his periodicals report it as hard fact! Yet the phantom hound of the Baskervilles was more real than the phantom hound of Baker Street. If Moriarty was still alive I might have suspected his twisted sense of humour of starting this hare – if a bloodhound can be so described.

The monograph on dogs may never have been written, though the subject must have been planned for inclusion in Holmes's *magnum opus, The Whole Art of Detection.* In his retirement he certainly wrote his *Practical Handbook of Bee Culture, with Some Observations upon the Segregation of the Queen*, and he may well have continued with the great treatise on detection between whiles. Bee-keepers have considerable time on their hands and Holmes could not tolerate mental inactivity after his abandonment of cocaine.

The monographs which he certainly completed while practising at Baker Street included no less than two on the subject of *The Human Ear,* both published in *The Anthropological Journal* in 1888. We have not succeeded in tracing these out-of-print numbers, but the several references to ears in his case indicate the areas he very likely developed. He would, of course, have pointed out the differences between male and female ears, a delicate auricle suggesting ivory or porcelain being contrasted with a red leathery conch bearing a thick tuft of hair in the intertragic notch. But he could not have cited the case of *The Cardboard Box,* for it did not occur until 1889, though in solving that problem he doubtless used knowledge which he had already published in his monographs.

This would have included his observation that 'there

is no part of the body which varies so much as the human ear. Each ear is as a rule quite distinctive, and differs from all other ones.' (Particuarly, of course, from the other ear on the same head, which would at least occur in reverse.) He recognized a family likeness in the ears of the two Misses Cushing, pointing out 'the same shortening of the pinna, the same broad curve of the upper lobe, the same convolution of the inner cartilage.' He also mentioned that male ears pierced for an ear-ring are most commonly found among seafaring men – and, of course, among people like Vincent Spaulding (alias John Clay, in *The Red-Headed League*), whose ears had been pierced by a gipsy when he was a lad.

These remarks show that he was well acquainted with the anatomy of the external ear, and we cannot doubt that the monographs described various characteristic forms of the helix, the tragus, the lobule, and 'Darwin's point'. He would also have reviewed the non-medical literature of the ear, if only to point out what a very inferior fellow Lombroso was. Lombroso published his theory of the 'born' criminal and how to recognize him by his features in 1875, but much had been written on criminal physiognomy since then. The monographs must at least have pointed out the fallacies in the beliefs that people with no free lobes have criminal tendencies, and that the ears of violent criminals are always large and stand out from the head.

The various theories published by physiognomists on small ears, large ears, round ears, pointed ears, sloping ears, red ears, thick ears, and so on, would have received short shrift from Holmes's pen. They would have been refuted by lithotypes of the wide, long lobes of Bismark's ears, the low position of Mr Gladstone's, the absence of lobes in Lord Leighton's, and many other such examples. One could wish to see what type of ear he found on Professor Moriarty and how it differed from his own. But he would surely have cited these features as aids to individual and family identifications, not as indications of moral tendencies.

Distorted and damaged ears would certainly have been accorded a large section. This would have included the use of frost-bite and childblains as clues, the nullifying effects of deerstalker caps, and the uses of cotton-wool. A stained plug of cotton-wool could be subjected to chemical analysis and a criminal identified by idiosyncrasies in the wax, but this technique would have been dragged in by Holmes's enthusiasm for chemistry rather than as a necessary procedure. (Today, however, it would be seriously considered, thus demonstrating how far ahead of his time was Holmes's thinking.)

His familiarity with the world of pugilism would have made him something of an expert on cauliflower ears, and the distortions of the female ear caused by heavy ear-rings cannot have escaped his notice. He could not, however, have referred to Dr Shlessinger's left ear, which was reported in the case of *Lady Frances Carfax* as 'jagged or torn,' because it was not until 1889 that 'Holy Peters' (as he was then called) was badly bitten in a saloon-fight at Adelaide. It is probable that Holmes was able to cite similar identifications by mutilated ears (with footnotes on Robert Jenkins and Van Gogh), and there were surely cases of criminal amputation earlier than those in *The Cardboard Box.* The fact that he had written *two* monographs on the human ear indicates that he had already made an exhaustive study of the subject by 1888.

On the afternoon of 27 September 1888, a little before Miss Mary Morstan called to consult Holmes about *The Sign of Four,* he confessed to Watson 'I have been guilty of several monographs,' and remarked that they were being translated into French by François le Villard, of the French detective service. He then produced three examples. One of these was *Upon the Distinction Between the Ashes of the Various Tobaccos,* in which 'I enumerate a hundred and forty forms of cigar, cigarette, and pipe tobacco, with coloured plates illustrating the difference in the ash.' This, he said, could be of supreme importance as a clue.

The second was *Upon the Tracing of Footsteps*, with some remarks upon the uses of plaster of Paris as a preserver of impresses, and the third *Upon the Influences of a Trade Upon the Form of the Hand,* with lithotypes of the hands of slaters, sailors, cork-cutters, compositors, weavers, and diamond-polishers. We know also, from the case of *The Solitary Cyclist,* that he was able to recognize and distinguish between the fingers of typists and pianists (see page 51), and was familiar with the knotted fists of pugilists like Steve Dixie, referred to jestingly in the report on *The Three Gables.* In *The Red-Headed League* Holmes deduces that Mr Jabez Wilson had done manual labour from the fact that his right hand was 'quite a size larger than the left', and in his account of *The Hound of the Baskervilles* Watson quotes Holmes as saying to Dr James Mortimer, 'I observe from your forefinger that you make your own cigarettes.'

Another monograph which Holmes had certainly written before 1898, because he referred to it in *The Dancing Men,* was *Upon Secret Writings,* 'in which I analyse one hundred and sixty separate ciphers.' If the hundred and sixty were all different *kinds* of cipher this monograph would probably still be the last word on the subject, for even acknowledged experts would have difficulty in finding anything like that number. It is likely, therefore, that most of them were variants of perhaps twenty basic types, taken from his cases by way of illustration. Unfortunately, Watson records only five cases in which ciphers are involved and, of these, neither the 'dancing men' nor the code used by Altamont to convey Naval 'secrets' to Von Bork could have been mentioned in the first edition of the monograph.

The earliest example we have was the message sent by Mr Beddoes to Mr Trevor in 1874, in the case of *The 'Gloria Scott'*. It read: 'The supply of game for London is going steadily up. Head-keeper Hudson, we believe, has been now told to receive all orders for fly-paper, and for preservation of your hen pheasant's life.' Mr Trevor, 'who was a fine, robust old man, was knocked clean down by it, as if it had been the butt-end of a pistol.' The key to this code is to read only every third word, starting with the first, and it must surely be the simplest non-symbolic code possible.

Since the monograph is on 'secret writings', the Musgrave Ritual must be regarded as the next example, though its cryptic message is hardly in code. However, in the missing lines of the Ritual quoted on page 83, the critical measurement is concealed in a mathematical enigma and the name of its originator is given in an anagram. The date of this investigation was 1879, and as Holmes was not in possession of these two clues they would not have appeared in the monograph. However, he undoubtedly dealt with the next recorded cipher in detail, both for its ingenuity and for the steps by which he deduced its meaning. This was the message sent to Holmes by Fred Porlock in 1888 and given in full by Watson in *The Valley of Fear.*

The original notion of picking out the words of the message in a well-known reference book and conveying them by the numbers of the pages and columns in which they occur was quite a masterpiece, but so also was the deductive process by which Holmes traced them without prior knowledge of the identity of the key volume. But this is not the place to quote the several pages it occupies in Watson's text, to which those not already familiar with it must be referred. As an anticlimax, Professor Moriarty's cryptic telegram at the end of *The Valley of Fear* might be cited as a sly kind of 'secret writing'. It said, simply, 'Dear me, Mr Holmes! Dear me!' It was a little crow of triumph without being a confession.

The remaining two ciphers recorded by Watson may have been included in later editions of the monograph if any were ever printed. They would certainly be added to the monograph material in the chapter on cryptograms in Holmes's *magnum opus* on *The Whole Art of Detection.* Both belong to the class of cipher based on arbitrary symbols, but in the first, that of the 'dancing men', the symbols stand merely for the letters of the alphabet, and in the second, for objects on the navy's secret list.

We can dismiss this second code in very few words, for we are given only three examples – namely, that 'sparking plugs' meant naval signals, a 'radiator' meant a battleship, and an 'oil-pump' a cruiser. It is quite impossible to crack an arbitrary code of this kind without the key. But when the symbols stand for the letters of English words it is possible to discover their meaning from the relative frequency with which the letters occur in the English language. Holmes gave the (descending) numerical order of their occurrence as:

E, T, A, O, I, N, S, H, R, D, L (etc)

Now, Mr William Legrand, in Edgar Allan Poe's *The Gold Bug,* solved a similar cipher on the assumption that the order of these same letters is:

E, A, O, I, D, H, N, R, S, T, . . . L (etc)

We decided to check this by the examination of a page in Robert Louis Stevenson's *Treasure Island,* as a fair sample of English, and found the order there to be:

E, T, A, O, H, S, N, I, R, D, L (etc)

From this we incline to believe that Holmes was more likely to be correct than Legrand, but then Holmes would doubtless say that Legrand, like Dupin, 'was a very inferior fellow'. In Legrand's cipher the letters were represented by random numbers, asterisks, brackets, etc, and they were not grouped into separate words. In Holmes's cipher the letters were represented by little 'matchstick' figures of dancing men, the one at the end of each word bearing a flag. This made Holmes's task the easier but, on the other hand, his material consisted of only twelve words, three of which were proper names, whereas Legrand had forty-eight words to play with. Perhaps they should be awarded equal marks.

We have notes on two more topics on which Holmes very likely wrote monographs, tattooing and malingering. There is, however a lack of information about his work on tattooing, though we know he had contributed to the literature on the subject by 1887. He said as much in Watson's account of *The Red-Headed League,* after mentioning the unique Chinese trick of staining fish-scales a delicate pink.

The other subject on which he said he had thought of writing a monograph, and most likely eventually did, is malingering. 'It is an art which is often useful,' he declared (in the case of *The Reigate Squires*) and in *The Priory School* we see a simple example when he pretended to sprain his ankle as a reason for asking Mr Reuben Hayes for a carriage – or a bicycle. Riding a bicycle with a sprained ankle is excruciatingly painful, but Mr Hayes may not have known this; or perhaps Holmes was only proposing to sit on it while Watson pushed him along.

Watson records several other cases in which Holmes practised some form of malingering, but the supreme example was, of course, deceiving Mr Culverton Smith, in *The Dying Detective,* that he was suffering from an obscure Asiatic disease. His delirious talk about half-crowns and oysters was not very convincing, but that was only for Watson's benefit; the rest of the charade went off perfectly.

The first case of malingering of which we have any record occurred in 1886 and is described in *The Resident Patient.* It will be remembered that Dr Trevelyan's mysterious visitor professed to suffer from catalepsy and succeeded in deceiving him although he was an acknowledged authority on the subject. But the report of it did not deceive Holmes, who had no hesitation in saying 'a fraudulent imitation, Watson, though I should hardly dare to hint as much to our specialist. It is a very easy complaint to imitate. I have done it myself.'

In the following year (in *A Scandal in Bohemia*) he

successfully deceived Miss Irene Adler that he was suffering from wounds and shock after getting knocked down by some squabbling loafers. It was, of course, a pre-arranged cod fight and, 'when the row broke out,' he explained afterwards, 'I had a little moist red paint in the palm of my hand. I rushed forward, fell down, clapped my hand to my face, and became a piteous spectacle. It is an old trick.' After they had carried him indoors and laid him on a couch, he motioned for air and so got them to open the window. It was a complete take-in, though the coachman 'was watching me narrowly.'

It was also in 1887 that he deceived the Reigate Squires by throwing a fit, and so prevented Inspector Forrester from giving the game away. 'My poor friend's face,' wrote Watson, 'had suddenly assumed the most dreadful expression. His eyes rolled upwards, his features writhed in agony, and with a suppressed groan he dropped on his face upon the ground. Horrified at the suddenness and severity of the attack, we carried him into the kitchen, where he lay back in a large chair and breathed heavily for some minutes.'

In the story of *The Empty House* we find Holmes disguised as an elderly deformed man. He was obliged to maintain his curved back until he decided to reveal his identity to Watson, when he declared, 'I am glad to stretch myself. It is no joke when a tall man has to take a foot off his stature for several hours on end.' But in the case of *The Illustrious Client* he managed to do his malingering by proxy, getting Watson to report the most serious symptoms to the press, suggesting that he was at death's door, when he was in fact recovering from two scalp wounds and some bruises with which 'his wiry constitution and his determined will were working wonders.' Another case of a man pretending to be suffering from crippling injuries was that of *The Man With the Twisted Lip* – Mr Neville St Clair, of Lee, in the county of Kent. No doubt Holmes would have drawn attention to the success of this ploy in his monograph, with possible reference to the hitherto unreported case of *The Amateur Mendicant Society*, referred to in *The Five Orange Pips*.

There is an important extension of the subject of malingering which would surely have warranted a second monograph. It might have been called *Upon the Use of False Obituaries in Crime and Detection, with Notes on the Concealment of Deaths.* It would have cited, as examples from his own cases, the reported murder of Mr Douglas, of Birlstone Manor House, in *The Valley of Fear*, and the near success of Mr Jonas Oldacre's bid for a tombstone in *The Norwood Builder.*

The supreme example of a false obituary was, of course, Sherlock Holmes's own reported death in the Reichenbach Falls in 1891. He maintained the deception by taking an extended sabbatical in Tibet and elsewhere under the name of Sigerson, and did not return until 1894. Whether this sort of thing can be called 'malingering' or not is a moot point, but he certainly should have included it. And there would surely have been a special section dealing with the reverse idea of making out that a dead person is still alive, as Sir Robert Norberton, of Shoscombe Old Place, did of his sister, Lady Beatrice Falder. Today, we might add the case of Sherlock Holmes himself, who is still presumed to flourish at the grand old age of a hundred and twenty-five.

4
Three Howlers

OF the three howlers to be reviewed, two were committed by that cold-blooded, 'desperate and dangerous' villain, Rodger Baskerville, alias Vandeleur, alias Stapleton, and the other by Dr Watson. Dr Watson's howler is of special interest because its effect has been to make Sherlock Holmes seem particularly dim-witted on an occasion when he was really remarkably astute. Holmes's apparent lapse has often been pointed out by readers of Watson's mistold version, and it is high time that the true facts were made known. But, first – Stapleton, as reported in *The Hound of the Baskervilles.*

Stapleton had no excuse for his mistakes, for not only did he profess to be, but he was, an accomplished student of natural history. Yet he lost his head when he first met Dr Watson by the great Grimpen Mire, on Dartmoor; his expert knowledge forsook him and he made the most absurd remarks. He was, however, a consummate actor and adequately covered his confusion, but it was fortunate for him that Watson's knowledge of both birds and insects was virtually nil.

He made his first mistake when 'a long, low moan, indescribably sad, swept over the moor. It filled the whole air. . . . From a dull murmur it swelled into a deep roar and then sank back into a melancholy throbbing murmur again.' It was, of course, the baying of

Stapleton's hound, but to put Watson off the scent he asked him if he had ever heard a bittern booming. When Watson said he had not, Stapleton mentioned that the bird was practically extinct in Engand and said he would not be surprised if 'what we have heard is the cry of the last of the bitterns.'

Now, any self-respecting naturalist would have been most surprised if it was that! To start with, the country of the bitterns was always East Anglia and, though an occasional non-breeding bird has been reported from other parts of the country, the 'last of the bitterns' would have been more than two hundred miles off-course if it were leaving Britain by way of Devonshire. According to James Fisher (*Bird Recognition,* vol. 2) the bittern was almost certainly extinct as a breeder in England between 1886 and 1911, and at the time of the Hound of the Baskervilles (1888) only a few winter visitors from the Continent were occasionally seen in Norfolk.

Then, the description of the sound heard on the moor is totally unlike the booming of a bittern. Watson described it on another occasion as 'a deep, muttered rumble, musical and yet menacing, rising and falling like the low, constant murmur of the sea.' But the sound made by the bittern is described by James Fisher as a 'penetrating *b'wump*', and by Peterson, Mountfort and Hollom (*A Field Guide to the Birds of Britain and Europe*) as beginning with two or three grunts, followed by an audible intake of breath and concluding with a loud, penetrating *woomp*! It is only necessary to say out loud, *grr-grr-ush-WOOMP*! to realize how absurd was Stapleton's reference to the bittern. Finally, if any doubt remains, the booming period of the bittern lasts from mid-January to mid-July and, according to

Watson's reports, the uncanny sound on Dartmoor was heard in late October.

Stapleton followed this gaffe with another, a few minutes later. He was evidently so greatly disturbed that his mind became totally unable to call correctly upon its knowledge of natural history. Still brooding over his unfortunate reference to the bittern, he said:

'"Yes, you will find some very singular points about the moor, Dr Watson. Oh, excuse me an instant. It is surely Cyclopides."'

'A small fly or moth had fluttered across our path, and in an instant Stapleton was rushing with extraordinary energy and speed in pursuit of it.'

Watson says he dodged from tuft to tuft in irregular zig-zags, for all the word like some huge moth himself, and we shall see that his jerky motion may be significant quite apart from the necessity of keeping to the islets of firm ground in the mire.

Now, there is no insect called Cyclopides, though there is a genus of flies called Cyclopodia. Unfortunately its members are all wingless, look like six-legged spiders, and are parasites on bats. Stapleton could not have chased one across the moor unless it were clinging to a bat, where he could not possibly have seen it anyway. Moreover, these flies are most commonly met with in Central America and are not at all likely to turn up in Devon.

However, Stapleton may have confused the name with Cyclorrhapha, a sub-order of flies containing several large British species and including the hover-flies, house-flies, blow-flies, and bot-flies. A brightly coloured hover-fly might well catch the eye of a naturalist, even when engrossed in a tricky conversation, and its darting, dodging flight, interspersed with brief stationary hovers, would compel a pursuer to make the 'jerky, zig-zag, irregular progress' that Watson records.

But the problem of the name remains, for no naturalist, even in the most desperate state, could ever refer to a single insect as a 'Cyclorrhapha'. The most likely explanation is that Stapleton ejaculated 'Cyclopides' merely as a means of breaking up the conversation, which had drifted dangerously towards the hound concealed on the moor. Any old name would have done and, having started with 'Cyclo-', he finished it off with what was simply an instinctive avoidance of '-rrhapha'. He was talking to a layman and it really did not matter, though Cyclopodia may also have been at the back of his mind.

Such looseness is admittedly understandable in a naturalist who, though having general interests, really specialized in the Lepidoptera, of which he thought his collection 'the most complete one in the south-west of England.' Further, the sudden appearance of a large hover-fly, which mimics a wasp or hornet, would have been especially likely to capture the attention of a preoccupied Lepidopterist for, though smaller, it fairly closely resembles the Hornet Clearwing moth (*Trochilium apiformis*). (*See* fig. 4.) Now, the Hornet Clearwing would be well worthy of notice on Dartmoor because it is usually found in flat meadow-land where osiers and poplars border the slow streams – a totally different type of country. Moreover, it is normally on the wing from the end of May to the end of July, and its fancied appearance on Dartmoor in October would certainly warrant a chase across the great Grimpen Mire.

In view of all this, there is a particularly fine touch in Stapleton's explanation to his wife as to why he was

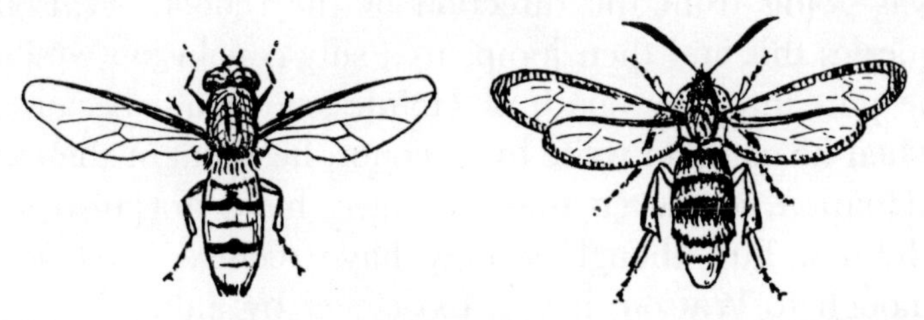

Fig. 4. 'A small fly or moth,' said Watson. *Left* :A Hover-fly. *Right* : The Hornet Clearwing moth. The similarity is plain, though in nature the moth is a little larger than the fly, but it would have been all one to Watson.

so hot. 'I was chasing a Cyclopides,' he panted. 'He is very rare, and seldom found in the late autumn. What a pity that I should have missed him!' It is indeed.

Dr Watson's howler is of a totally different order. It had to do with logic, not with knowledge, and it in no way reflected on his professional skill as a story-teller. However, as a good writer should, he re-lives the dramatic episodes as he recounts them and, in the excitement of a thrilling moment, he is inclined to jump to conclusions to enhance the effcct – even when they are not strictly justified. Occasionally this leads him into gross error and there is a particularly good example of this in his account of the Priory School case. In missing out an important passage in Holmes's interpretation of the cycle tracks on Lower Gill Moor, he commits a solecism which could have done no good to the great detective's reputation. However, the circumstances of the case very fortunately enable the missing passage to be reconstructed and the proper deductions from the cycle tracks to be drawn.

In Watson's account, while they are examining the track of the bicycle with Dunlop tyres Holmes remarks, 'This track, as you perceive, was made by a rider who was going from the direction of the school.' Watson queries this and then jumps to a silly conclusion which he puts into the mouth of Holmes, no doubt because, when he came to write his account, he thought the explanation so clever that he must have got it from Holmes. But, though it may have seemed 'obvious' enough to Watson, it was too clever by half.

According to Watson's account, Holmes, after the statement just quoted, goes on without a break to point out that the more deeply sunk impression is made by the back wheel, and this is confirmed because it clearly crosses over the other impression. Watson thought this showed Holmes the direction of travel, but of course it could do nothing of the sort. The back wheel would follow the front whichever way the machine were going. No, Holmes was simply ascertaining which of the two tyres bore 'the patch upon the outer cover', a fact which might be invaluable later in making an identification.

However, Watson, full of his bright idea, ignores this point entirely and forgets altogether the reasons actually given by Holmes for believing that the bicycle 'was undoubtedly heading away from the school.' The missing passage should, of course, have followed immediately after these words.

Before attempting to reconstruct the passage we should draw attention to a fact stated later in Watson's narrative, but which must have been patent at the outset of the expedition. This is that the moor was not only covered with heather, but also with scattered patches of gorse. Herr Heidegger's body was found in a gorse bush, it will be remembered, and we were told early on that the moor was 'intersected with a thousand sheep-paths', which must have threaded their way

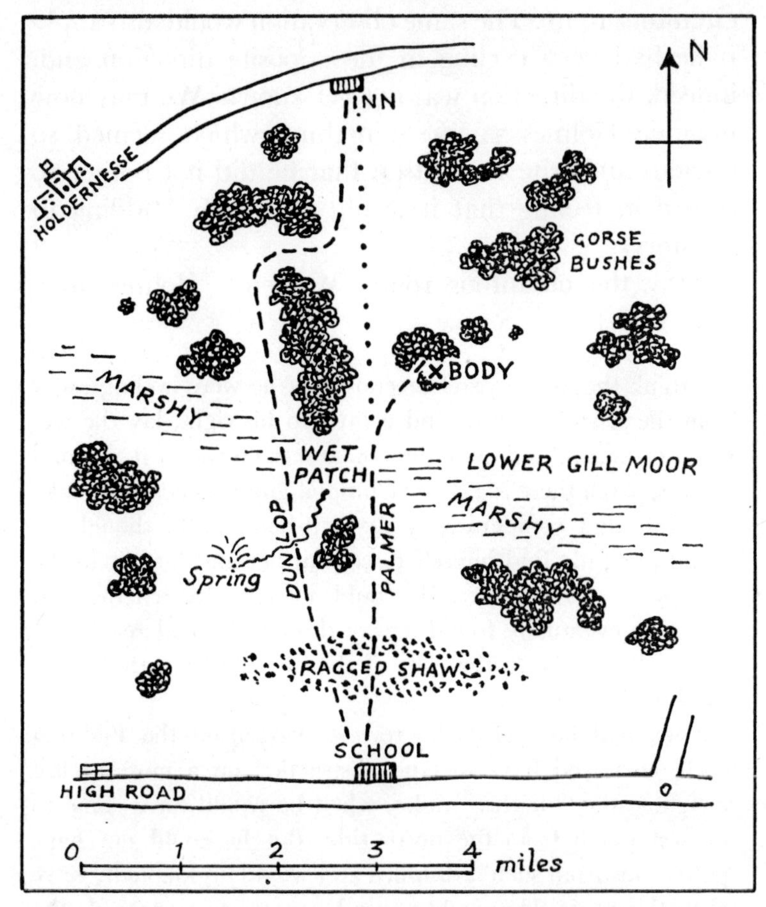

Fig. 5. Lower Gill Moor, showing the distribution of the gorse bushes and the tracks of the bicycles. (Adapted from a sketch by John H. Watson.)

through the gorse where gaps occurred.

A glance at the sketch-map in figure 5 shows that the Dunlop tyre tracks followed a path or paths which would have taken the rider to a point about midway between Holdernesse Hall and the Fighting Cock inn. That is, nearly two miles from either of them, and if either was the cyclist's goal he was following a very circuitous route. The same observation would also apply if he had been cycling in the opposite direction and, indeed, the direction was not yet known. We may now imagine Holmes saying something which seemed so obvious and trite to Watson that he did not bother to record it, feeling that it would be merely padding in his story.

Why the circuitous route, Watson? [Holmes may have said.]

I think the answer is clear enough if he were cycling away from the school. Ahead, and a little to his right, lay the wet patch of marsh, and even the cow tracks go round it. Beyond the wet patch there is a dense clump of gorse, so he would take the clear and comparatively dry left-hand path, though he would presently find himself forced farther and farther to the west by the gorse bushes. He could not have forseen this and before he eventually found a way through he had reached a point fully a mile to the west of the bee-line from the school to the Fighting Cock.

Now, had he cycled the reverse way, *from* the Fighting Cock, he would have met no obstruction on a more or less straight course for three miles, when he would have come to the wet patch from the north side. But he could not have spotted this from such a distance and would undoubtedly have taken this route. He would never have set out to encircle the gorse to the west, for this would have taken him right out of his way for no reason. Yet the cyclist was definitely on that route, Watson, so we may safely deduce that he was heading away from the school, not towards it.

Holmes was using a large ordnance map, but our sketch-map is adapted from the one provided by Watson, with some irrelevant details omitted and the gorse bushes added. The deduced routes followed by the bicycles have been completed and the direct route from the school to the inn is shown by a dotted line. A scale has also been provided, for the necessarily exaggerated sizes of the roads and buildings cause the distances to appear much diminished. It is six miles from the school to the inn, according to Watson, and Ragged Shaw is nearly two miles long.

With regard to the bicycle with Palmer tyres, Holmes assumed that it had been ridden in the same general northerly direction as the other one, and he was very soon proved correct by the discovery of Heidegger's body. The tracks showed that Heidegger had emerged from Ragged Shaw at a more easterly point than the Dunlop-tyred cycle, and had made to pass the wet patch in the marsh on the right-hand side. However, he was almost immediately chased by the ruffian Reuben Hayes, on the horse fitted with shoes shaped like a cow's cloven hoofs. He was caught as he crossed the marshy tract and collapsed into a gorse bush. But for this attack he would have made a clear, direct run across the moor to the Fighting Cock, but then nobody could have deduced from his tracks whether he was coming or going.

Yet Herr Heidegger's fatal ride provides confirmation of the important part played by the gorse bushes in this case. From his bedroom window he had seen young Lord Saltire ride off on his bicycle and, after partly dressing, he had taken out his own machine to give chase. But by that time Lord Saltire was out of sight, hidden by the westerly mass of gorse bushes, and this alone accounts for Heidegger's continuing along the other route.

It is true that the head of a boy on a bicycle might be visible over a clump of ordinary moorland gorse, but a dip in the ground could take him momentarily out of sight. In any case, a boy's head would appear very small indeed at a distance of a mile and, as is common with young riders, he was very likely bent low over the handlebars. Watson evidently failed to realize the general importance of the gorse. Had he done so, we should not have felt it desirable to supply the missing passage to his narrative.

5
The Musgrave Muddle

THE story of *The Musgrave Ritual* contains a great many debatable details, but the term 'muddle' does not refer to them but to the multifarious published criticisms of them. Not that it is intended to review the criticisms – heaven forbid! – but rather to clarify the points at issue and contribute a new discovery, with the hope that some of the muddle will evaporate.

The seventeenth-century Ritual gives cryptic instructions for the discovery of a hidden treasure, but the vital clue depends upon the positions of two trees, an oak and an elm. The oak is used to indicate the position of the sun when the shadow of the elm points to a spot on the ground from which certain measurements are to be taken, but these are, to say the least, remarkable. According to the Ritual they are to be made by taking twenty paces to the north, ten to the east, four to the south and two to the west, but these last two enter the door of the house. Now, the door was said by Holmes to be in the centre of the wall, so that the house was apparently less than eight paces wide! It is clear that the whole of the evidence, as recorded by Watson, needs careful checking, beginning with the two trees.

The oak presents no problems, as a tree, but its situation is important for fixing the date and time of day for applying the Ritual. We note, however, that it was a 'magnificent tree' with 'a girth of 23 feet', and that it stood 'right in front of the house, upon the left-hand side of the drive'. It could certainly have been there at the time of the Norman Conquest, as Reginald Musgrave stated, and still be flourishing eight hundred years later when Sherlock Holmes saw it. Its height is of no importance provided that the sun can be seen over it – at any distance over it – at the right time and from the right place.

It is, however, likely to have been at least 80 feet high, for it was a notable tree with a trunk more than two yards in diameter.* We are not told where the right place of observation is, though this is obviously important. It cannot have been some point out in the grounds or its position would have been indicated. It may be assumed that the most natural place would have been from the steps of the original front door. The observation is unlikely to have been made through the crude, distorting, and possibly stained small panes of the mullioned windows, and there is no suggestion that it was made from the roof. The lack of direction to some special site leaves us no alternative but to accept the obvious one.

So much for the place of observation, but we also need to know the position of the oak. We are told that it was nearly twice as far from the house as the elm, but whereas this could mean in a straight line through the elm to meet the centre of the house at right-angles, it could also mean that Holmes found he had to walk about as far again from the elm to the house as he did

* 'Oak attains a height of 60–100 ft according to soil and locality. The diameter is about 4–6 ft, although in exceptional trees it may be considerably more.' – *A Handbook of Hardwoods,* Forest Products Research, HMSO, 1956.

from the oak to the elm, the two journeys not necessarily being in the same straight line – or even in perfectly straight lines at all.

Since the oak is unlikely to have been less than 80 feet high its shadow was probably at least 120 feet long. This follows from the method used to calculate the height of the elm, to be described shortly. The oak must therefore have been at a greater distance than this from the house (in the direction of its shadow) or the observer would have been within its shadow and unable to see the sun over it. So that when Holmes said that the oak stood 'right in front of the house' he clearly meant that it blocked the centre of his view of the house as he came up the drive; it must have been at least 40 yards away from the house – not literally 'right in front'.

The elm tree raises more problems than the oak, in spite of – or because of – the fact that we are told more about it. For one thing, it was 64 feet high when the boy Reginald Musgrave measured it with his tutor in about 1869. The only reason given for felling this tree soon afterwards is that it was struck by lightning, so it was presumably in a healthy enough state. But if it was used to draw up the Ritual about 1650, how did it manage to remain exactly 64 feet high for 220 years?

The common English elm grows from 120 to 150 feet high, according to the *Handbook of Hardwoods* cited above, and lives for about three hundred years. The Musgrave elm was alive when struck by lightning so that it can hardly have been more than sixty or seventy years old in 1650. It should have continued growing, but since it was required to remain at 64 feet for the purposes of the Ritual it must have been lopped at regular intervals.

Now, if the Ritual were to remain valid for any considerable number of years it must have contained, or been accompanied by, instructions – implicit or explicit – for periodic lopping. The act itself would have had a ceremonial character and, though its purpose would have been kept secret, knowledge of it must have been passed on because the height of the tree had been faithfully preserved right up to 1869. How can we account for this?

The most probable answer would appear to be that a piece of the Ritual is missing and that when Brunton, the butler, 'thrust into his breast the chart-like paper which he had originally been studying', he inadvertently shoved in with it a scrap of manuscript detached from the mouldy old document described by Reginald Musgrave as 'nothing of any importance at all'. Musgrave would obviously never have missed it, or cared much if he had, but it was, of course, part of the Ritual. The missing piece would appear to be lost, but it may be the fragment of yellowed parchment which fluttered out of a pauper's grave (possibly Brunton's) when it was accidentally sliced off during a road-widening operation beside the Hurlstone village burial-ground. If so, the complete version of the Ritual reads as follows:

Whose was it?
His who is gone.
Who shall have it?
He who will come.
What was the month?
The sixth from the first.
Where was the sun?
Over the oak.
Where was the shadow?

Under the elm.
Who gauged the bole?
He shall not be named.
Come, what was his name?
Haw! I am very ill.
What was the measure?
The square and the cube.
How shall we keep it?
By obtruncation.
When shall we do it?
At five and by five of the day of his death.
Who shall be punished?
He who misjudges.
How was it stepped?
North by ten and by ten, east by five and by five, south by two and by two, west by one and by one, and so under.
What shall we give for it?
All that is ours.
Why should we give it?
For the sake of the trust.

Internal evidence that the additional lines are genuine has been found both in the curious answer to the demand for the name of the man who measured the height of the tree, and in the statement of the height itself. Not only does 'Haw! I am very ill' suggest that a doctor is wanted, but the line itself provides the doctor: it is a simple anagram of 'William Harvey', Charles I's personal physician and discoverer of the circulation of the blood. It is understandable that the doctor should not wish his name to be used, and his wish is duly recorded, but those who drew up the Ritual determined to have it in somehow as a guarantee of reliability, for Harvey was already famous as a meticulously careful scientist.

Again, 'The square and the cube' can have but one plausible interpretation: it represents a number which is both a square and a cube. The only applicable number of this kind is 64, which is the square of 8 and the cube of 4. Now, we already know that 64 is the correct answer, so this is either an unbelievable coincidence or the line is a genuine part of the Ritual.*

'At five and by five of the day of his death' suggests that the height of the tree was maintained by a sort of beheading ceremony every ten – or perhaps twenty-five – years on the anniversary of the beheading of Charles I. This would not have seemed ghoulish but rather the opposite, for the point would obviously have been the fact that the tree continued to live and grow in spite of it.

However, none of these missing lines was essential to the practical interpretation of the Ritual. Sherlock Holmes, knowing that the elm was 64 feet high, determined the length of its shadow by a simple experiment. He took a fishing-rod six feet long and, standing it upright on the ground, noted that it cast a shadow nine feet long. From this it was a simple matter to calculate that an elm tree 64 feet high would cast a shadow 96 feet long. But to get the measurement with the rod correct Holmes should have made sure that the sun was over the oak from the point of view of a man standing on the step of the house, and he does not seem to have done this.

When he decided he would have to wait nearly an hour before the sun would be over the oak, Holmes was standing somewhere near the elm, for that was where Musgrave took him 'at once, without our entering the house'. Had he been on the step of the house

* Consider these alternatives and you will find you have no real choice.

the sun would have appeared over the oak a little earlier (had it been in the morning) than he would have estimated from the elm, and certainly not quite so high in the sky, but these small differences must have been fortuitously corrected by such details as Holmes's own height compared with the original Musgrave's, his failure to hold the fishing-rod absolutely upright, a slight local rise in the ground where the rod's shadow was measured, or the time taken to measure out the hypothetical shadow of the elm. There was certainly an element of luck in his final arrival at the right spot from which to pace out the directions given in the Ritual.

Holmes's first observation that the sun was low in the sky but would presently be above the oak surely implies that it was in the morning, but it need not have been very early. Ashdown Forest rose to 700 feet roughly towards the east and the sun could have been a fair way on its journey yet still appear 'low' over the high Forest Ridge, especially if it was late in the year. Or Hurlstone Manor itself may have been at the bottom of a fairly deep valley.

It is true that Holmes told Watson that when Musgrave consulted him, 'the same afternoon saw us at Hurlstone', but this can be explained without supposing that they spent a night in the house before making their experiments, though this also is a possibility. Holmes distinctly says that they went to work in the grounds directly they arrived – and that is, in fact, the explanation! Hurlstone was the name of the house. They spent the entire morning in the grounds, not actually arriving at the house itself until past mid-day. That this was so is evident from Holmes's description of the house, which he relates exactly as if he had examined it directly he arrived there – in the afternoon.

Although it was in the morning, then, that the experiments were apparently made, it could not have been very early. It was the same morning that Musgrave had called upon Holmes in London and stated his problem, after which they had taken 'the first train down to Sussex'. In those days many people habitually rose very early. Ruskin, for example, always rose before dawn, even in the summer, and did an hour's work before breakfast, and many others could be cited. So we are free to suppose that Musgrave had stayed overnight in London and called upon Holmes at about half-past seven and got him out of bed (unless he had been working all night). It could not have taken Musgrave more than half an hour to state his problem (it takes less than twenty minutes to read aloud Holmes's verbatim report of the interview), for they had to catch a train which would get them to Hurlstone by, at the latest, half past nine. We know this because it took nearly one hour for the sun to move from its position 'low in the heavens' to its place over the oak and, as we shall see, this cannot have been later than about a quarter past ten.

The time of the day depended on both the altitude of the sun and the month of the year, and the first is given by Holmes's experiment with the fishing-rod. To cast the observed shadow on level ground the sun must have been between 33 and 34 degrees above the true horizon, and we have no reason whatever to suppose that the ground was not more or less level. The Ritual itself gives the month of the year as 'the sixth from the first', but it is certainly debatable whether the 'first' was the month of January or the period between 25 March and 25 April.

The old Roman calendar began the year in March, New Year's Day being 25 March for a very long time. Julius Caesar changed the New Year to 1 January but in Christendom 25 March was adopted for ecclesiastical reasons (connected with Easter). In England the 1 January again became the New Year's Day at the time of the Norman Conquest, but the 25 March was re-established to keep in line with the Roman Church. The revision of the calendar by Pope Gregory XIII in 1582 set back New Year's Day to 1 January yet once more, and Scotland followed suit in 1600, but England retained 25 March because it was now a Protestant country and would not follow the example of a pope. Nevertheless, many people felt about it much as we do today about 5 April as the first day of the Fiscal Year: it was a legal fiction.

Samuel Pepys, for example, who was a Protestant, not only began the first year of his diary on the 1 January 1660, but all through his life regarded this as New Year's Day. His diary for 31 December 1662, begins: 'Thus ends this year with great mirth to me and my wife.' On 31 December 1665, he writes: 'Thus ends this year, to my great joy, in this manner. I have raised my estate from 1300 *l.* in this year to 4400 *l.*' And again, on 31 December 1667: 'Thus ends the year, with great happiness to myself and family.' (His annual merry-making on 26 March had nothing to do with the new year; it celebrated the day 'that I was cut for the stone at Mrs Turner's in Salisbury Court.' But this is hardly relevant.)

The official change back to 1 January did not take place in England until 1752, though in order not to upset financial accounting 25 March was, in principle, retained for fiscal purposes – but with a difference. In changing to the Gregorian calendar, eleven days were omitted from the year 1752 for purely astronomical reasons, so eleven days had to be added to 25 March to maintain the fiscal year at full strength. This made the fiscal New Year's Day 5 April.* In considering how the Musgraves regarded the New Year a full century earlier, we should realize that they are as likely as not to have had the same views as people like Samuel Pepys.

So the Ritual's 'first' month could have been either January or the odd period from 25 March to 25 April. We have to consider both, treating them as independent cases, but we should not try to be too particular as to the *exact* dates for we do not know what is meant by 'the sixth from the first'. The sixth month counting *from* January would be July, for example, but the sixth month of a year starting *with* January is June. Further, we are not told whether to reckon from the first day of the month, its middle, or its end.

If we decide that the month is either June or July, the end of June might prove near enough, for 21 June is the summer solstice. If we take 25 March as New Year's Day, then the sixth month would begin on either 25 August or 25 September, and we might feel again that some middle date would be the best bet. So much is left to guesswork in the Ritual that precise computations can only be a waste of time, but we may expect that the middle points should give us a rough but reasonable idea of what must have taken place in each case. We may then be able to decide which is more probable from other evidence – if we can resolve certain apparent inconsistencies.

So we shall consider two broad cases: first, that the

* For a time it became 6 April, again for astronomical reasons, but it is now back on the fifth.

'sixth from the first' is best treated as somewhere around the summer solstice, namely 21 June, and second that, alternatively, it may be taken as very approximately represented by 1 September. We shall designate these cases as 'June' and 'Sept.' respectively.

Now, each of these two cases must again be subdivided according to whether we believe that Holmes made his measurements in the morning or the afternoon. Reasons have already been given for supposing they were made in the morning, but many 'historians' consider that Watson made a slip in reporting Holmes and that the afternoon is more likely. We shall, in fact, find that while the Sept. case is open to either morning or afternoon interpretations, the June case can be justified only as an afternoon event. In both cases the house, with its new wing, is 'L-shaped' as described, though in Sept. the L has to be reversed (=⅃) if the new wing is to make the longer arm. (It should be noted that a reversed L is still a kind of L.)

To take the Sept. case first, at this time of the year the sun is about 33 degrees above the horizon at around ten in the morning when it is a little to the south of south-east, and at two in the afternoon, when it is a little to the south of south-west. Figure 6 shows a possible disposition of the house, the elm, and the oak, for some time between ten and ten-fifteen in the morning, though the plan can easily be modified to suit times a little outside these limits. The oak would appear in front of the whole house (including the new wing) to anybody coming up the drive, as Holmes stated.

This plan could not be adapted to suit the afternoon time of two o'clock, for if the shadow of the elm and the sunbeam over the oak are drawn to the south-west instead of the south-east, the oak could not possibly

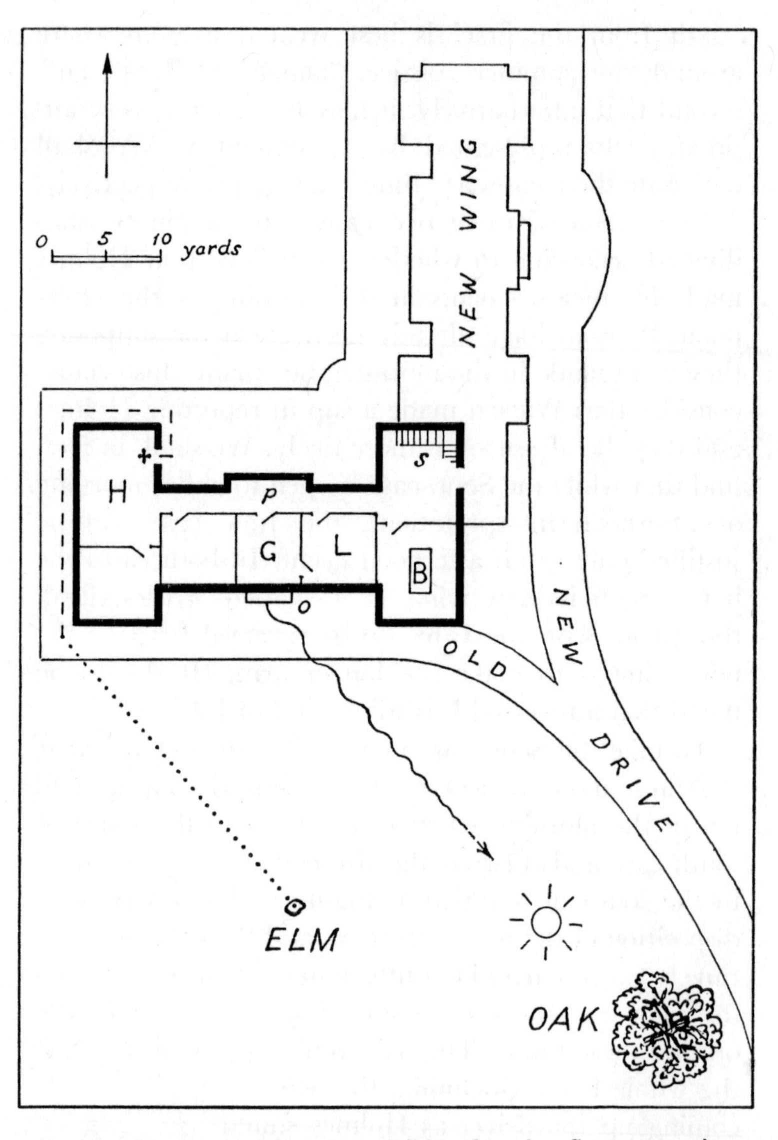

Fig. 6. Hurlstone Manor: possible plan for Sept., morning. H, Hall. G, Gun-room. L, Library. B, Full-sized billiard table in billiard-room. *s*, Stairs. *p*, Passage. *o*, Original main entrance. Dotted line: shadow of elm. Broken line: paced measurements of the Ritual. Wavy line: direction of sun over the oak.

appear to be in front of the house however the drive were placed. This is because the new wing must remain at the eastern end of the old building if the pacings described in the Ritual are to lead to the right door in the middle of the right wall. An alternative plan possible for two o'clock is given in Figure 7, but in this the layout of the house and the new wing has to be differently orientated.

As for the other case, in June the sun has an altitude of about 33 degrees around either eight in the morning when the sun is approximately due east, or four in the afternoon, when it is approximately due west. Figure 8 is a plan suitable for the afternoon, but it has proved impossible to devise a credible plan for the morning time because, in the morning, the shadow of the elm would have to lie to the east of the house, no matter how it is drawn, and the pacing 'north by ten and by ten' must lie along a western wall. It might be thought possible to adapt the afternoon scheme to a house disposed as in Figure 6, but this will not do because first, the elm would then come close to the front wall and the oak could not be placed less than twice as far away, and second, because of Holmes's announcement that following the shadow led them nearly *to* the wall. But, apart from these considerations, Holmes and Musgrave could not have got down to Hurlstone by eight o'clock in the morning!

The conclusion, then, is that Holmes's investigation at Hurlstone could have taken place in late June or early July in the afternoon, at about 4 o'clock, or in late August or early September in either the morning soon after 10 o'clock, or the afternoon at around 2 o'clock. Considerable latitude may be allowed for the position of the exact date for all these times are ap-

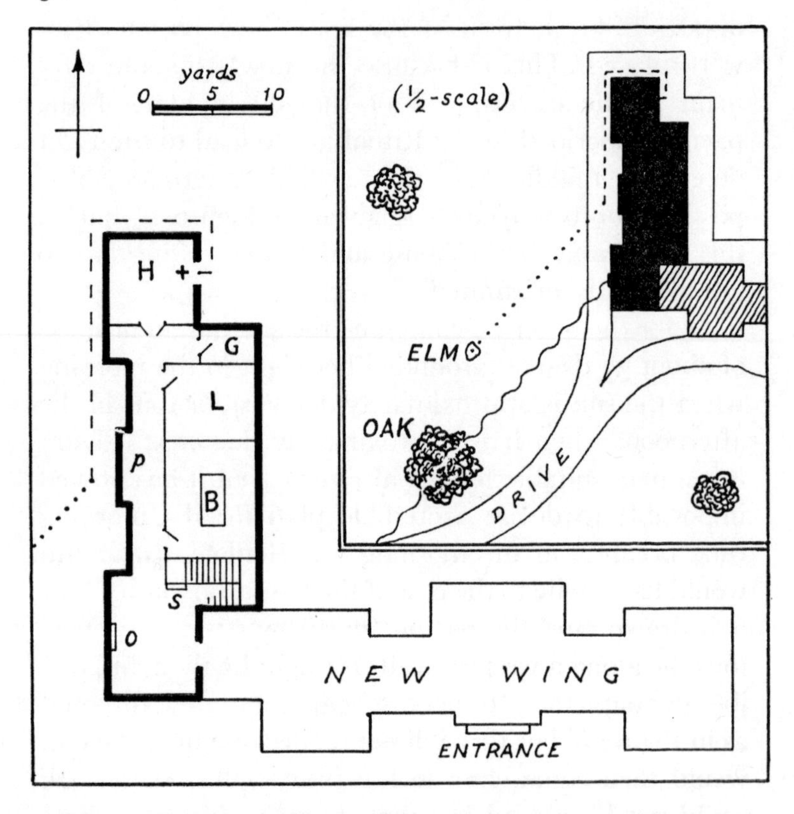

Fig. 7. Hurlstone Manor: possible plan for Sept., afternoon. H, Hall, G, Gun-room. L, Library, B, Full-sized billiard table in billiard-room. *s,* Stairs. *p,* Passage. *o,* Original main entrance. Dotted line: shadow of elm. Broken line: paced measurements of the Ritual: Wavy line: direction of sun over the oak. *Note*: The distance between the elm and the oak should be about double that shown, the oak being moved down the wavy line and the curve of the drive adjusted.

proximate, but the *general* direction of the shadows is not seriously altered even if we are a week or two out. There is more scope here in June, however, because in the late afternoon the sun's motion is largely vertical, whereas in September, during the few possible hours

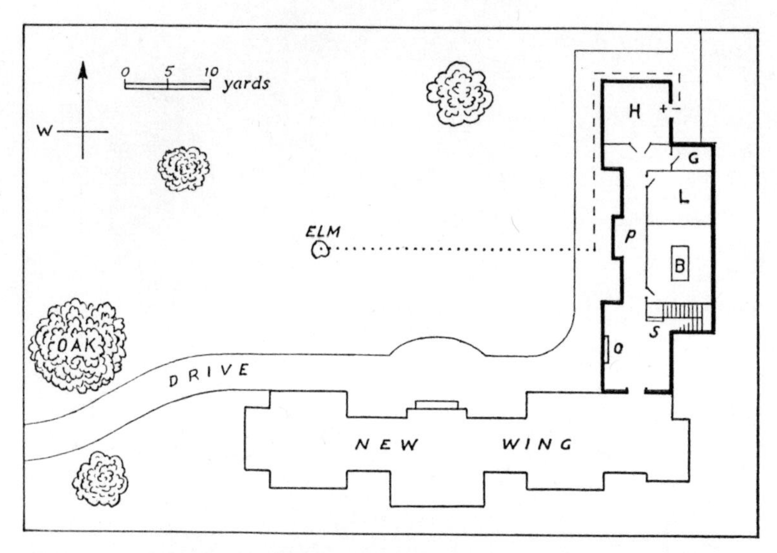

Fig. 8. Hurlstone Manor: possible plan for June, afternoon. H, Hall. G, Gun-room. L, Library. B, Full-sized billiard table in billiard-room. *s*, Stairs. *p*, Passage. *o*, Original main entrance. Dotted line: shadow of elm. Broken line: paced measurements of the Ritual.

on either side of midday, it is chiefly horizontal.

The plan of the house and grounds depends entirely on which of the three possible times is chosen, but only the morning time in early September can really be made to accommodate Holmes's first observations on his arrival at Hurlstone without contradicting any of his other statements – unless Watson reported him incorrectly.

6
Three Letters

ANY authentic addition to the records of the late Mr Sherlock Holmes and his associates will be welcomed by students of the history of detection. At least two such additions have come to light through a careful and detailed study of the document known as *Codex C-D.* This comprises several papers bearing the name of Dr Watson's literary agent, Mr Arthur Conan Doyle, who was knighted in 1902 though not, for some reason, for his services to Dr Watson. Doyle also wrote up a few case histories of unusual crimes himself, though he was meticulously careful not to trespass on Watson's own field. However, he did quote Sherlock Holmes's opinion on at least one case in which Holmes was not officially engaged and which Watson therefore did not chronicle. This has been noted before by others, but it is outlined again here because of its relevance in the sequel.

According to Doyle, Holmes expressed his views of this case in a letter to *The Times,* which he began by repeating one of his most celebrated *dicta* – one which Watson himself records more than once and which is surely as good as the great man's signature or thumbprint. Watson's agent, anxious not to tread on his client's preserves, scrupulously refrains from mentioning Holmes by name, but so well known is this saying that nobody else would have dared to use it without acknowledgement, nor would *The Times* have printed it except in a letter from Holmes himself. However, the third letter to be considered here suggests that it did not appear in *The Times* at all, and this is borne out by the fact that no copy of the edition of *The Times* in which the letter is said to have appeared has been traced.

The letter is quoted in a report entitled *The Lost Special,* which describes the mysterious disappearance of a special train in south Lancashire on 3 June 1890, a year familiar to readers of Dr Watson's chronicles as that of the singular business of *The Red-headed League. The Lost Special* (in *The Conan Doyle Stories*) concerned a special train commissioned at Liverpool to take a Monsieur Caratal and his companion to London after they had missed the express. The special had a clear run as far as Manchester but never arrived, yet there had been no accident on the line and no train had been observed on any of the four branch lines leading off to various iron works and collieries.

The train seemed to have completely vanished and many fanciful attempts to explain its disappearance were made by newspapers and private individuals. However, one sensible suggestion, said to have appeared in *The Times* on 3 July 'over the signature of an amateur reasoner of some celebrity at that date, attempted to deal with the matter in a critical and semi-scientific manner.' This suggestion began with the familiar words: 'It is one of the elementary principles of practical reasoning that when the impossible has been eliminated the residuum, *however improbable,* must contain the truth.'

Well, there it is! – the unmistakable voice of the

Master, but a quotation, nevertheless. He goes on to argue the case and points out how the investigation should proceed. In spite of the fact that some surprise evidence knocks the bottom out of all the current theories of the mystery, the advice of the celebrated amateur reasoner turns out to be excellent and leads to the correct solution.

It may be objected that Holmes could hardly have been called an 'amateur' in 1890, but there can be little doubt that this is how he was regarded by the public. He openly professed to despise the professionals and officials, and was known to attach little importance to the size of his fees, sometimes even waiving them altogether. He may be justly described as an amateur who needs to have his expenses paid – provided it be recognized that a reasonable livelihood is a relevant, and indeed essential, item of anybody's expenses.

In his account of another affair, under the title of *The Man With the Watches,* Watson's literary agent also quoted from a letter in a newspaper by a 'well-known criminal investigator', but this was alleged to have appeared in the *Daily Gazette*. Sherlock Holmes has been named by more than one writer as the author of this letter, too, and it has even been ascribed, by Martin Dakin, to his brother Mycroft. However, both these identifications are very doubtful and there is a much more plausible alternative.

That Holmes did not write it is not evident from the fact that he was in Tibet in 1892, when the puzzling events occurred, for the mystery remained unsolved for at least five years and the letter may have appeared at any time up to 1897. The report is not definitive in the matter of the date, but the chief objection to believing that Holmes wrote the letter lies in its substance. It begins as follows:

Whatever may be the truth, it must depend upon some bizarre and rare combination of events, so we need have no hesitation in postulating such events in our explanation. In the absence of data we must abandon the analytic or scientific method of investigation, and must approach it in the synthetic fashion. In a word, instead of taking known events and deducing from them what has occurred, we must build up a fanciful explanation if it will only be consistent with known events.

Now, it is scarcely credible that Holmes, who declared that 'the temptation to form premature theories upon insufficient data is the bane of our profession', and who more than once pointed out to Watson 'how dangerous it always is to reason from insufficient data,' ever gave such advice to anybody. Yet the writer of the letter has *no hesitation* in doing what Holmes deliberately said is *always dangerous*! Such advice runs absolutely counter to Holmes's stated principles and seems much more likely to have proceeded from the sort of man who would loiter about the streets wearing grey-tinted sun-glasses and a Masonic tie-pin – in short, Barker, 'my hated rival upon the Surrey shore.'

In fact, the advice exactly describes Barker's method of work as revealed in the case of *The Retired Colourman.* Here, Holmes says of Barker, 'we have been working independently', but also 'he has done nothing save what I told him.' This last is, of course, a 'Sherlockism'. Holmes, working independently, would have told him nothing; therefore Barker had done nothing worth mentioning at all! How, then, had he 'been interesting himself also' in Josiah Amberley's business? Obviously along 'synthetic' lines, thinking up 'fanciful explanations' in the 'absence of data'.

Thus, Barker is clearly the most likely candidate for the authorship of the letter. Of the other investigators of this period known to Watson's literary agent, it could hardly have been Inspector Hopkins of Scotland Yard, or Inspector Baynes of the Surrey Constabulary, for police officers are not permitted to air their views in letters to the newspapers. But if Barker were interested this is just what he would be most likely to do, for the 'Rugby Mystery', as it came to be called, touched London only at Euston Station and Barker's stamping ground lay south of the Thames. And it must be admitted that his method is ideally suited to the investigation, in South London, of events occurring somewhere in the middle of England.

So much for the first two letters. They purport to have been quoted by Watson's agent in literary efforts of his own, and our third letter does suggest that Doyle pumped Watson and perhaps others for information which he used without acknowledgement; otherwise it is impossible to account for the letter in *The Lost Special* which he rashly pretends appeared in *The Times.* He probably made it up himself from Watson's almost *verbatim* report to him of Holmes's view of the matter. On the other hand, Barker's letter may indeed be genuine and have appeared in the *Daily Gazette.* At all events, it is now beyond reasonable doubt that Doyle was the author of both *The Lost Special* and *The Man With the Watches,* for this is virtually stated in a letter almost certainly addressed to Doyle, of which we have the original manuscript.*

* Conan Doyle's reply to this letter would have been of great interest, apart from the fact that it would prove that Doyle had received it – a matter about which we cannot be certain.

Watson's (These travelling ink-pots!) wound, which he
received on ~~the~~ the North West Frontier. You at least
acknowledge that he referred to it sometimes as
affecting his shoulder, and at others his leg, but
are at a loss to account for this inconsistency.

I can assure you there is no inconsistency and,
further, that he was not wounded on two occasions but only one.
The fact is, as he himself explained to me, the Jezail
bullet came from a sniper when he was in the act
of ~~putting~~ pulling at his boot after getting his
foot caught in a rocky fissure. He was, at that
moment, completely doubled up and the bullet
glanced off his ankle-bone [nicking his Achilles tendon] to pass beneath his
collar-bone and lodge in his shoulder. He was thus
shot in the front, not in the back, but the
ludicrousness of his position has prevented his
elaborating on a matter really quite irrelevant to

Fig. 9. Facsimile of part of Mr Trample Cloisture's letter to Conan Doyle.

This letter is reported to have been found several years ago screwed up and badly soiled in a sack of waste paper on a rubbish-heap. The finder, who has not since been traced, was a kind of itinerant collector of old bottles, which he sold as curios or antiques. His favourite hunting-places were country rubbish-tips, but he was unable to say where this particular item turned up, except that he was 'doing' the Tunbridge Wells area at the time. He said that he often had to hunt around for packing paper to prevent the bottles in his haversack clinking together, and the possible interest of this letter struck him quite by chance during a turn-out several weeks later. He seems to have parted with the letter in exchange for a scotch egg and a shandy-gaff in one of the two 'Bell' inns on the Maidstone-Rochester road, and here is its text in full:

As from the Old Club.
(I shall have no address
until I arrive home.)

Friday

My dear Arthur,

May I congratulate you on your two essays at the detective story – a literary form in which you have for so long, and so successfully acted as agent for John Watson? I am sure your services to Watson should not prevent your trying your own hand in this field, and your fears that some may regard this as a breach of etiquette are groundless. Although the cases you report (I refer to the *Special* and the *Watches*. Have you written any others?) were mentioned in the Press at the time they occurred, and seem to have come to the notice of Mr Sherlock Holmes, Watson has not bothered to record them because Holmes was not officially engaged in either. Thus, you are certainly not treading on his toes and surely need not have bothered to change the names of the persons and places involved. Indeed, my only criticism is that the locale you have chosen is, perhaps, not entirely appropriate, and you would have done better to *invent* a newspaper than to cite *The Times*, whose files may be searched in vain for your alleged report.

Please excuse this scrawl, but I am writing this in the train from Edinburgh and, since I have another two hours of journey before me, may I animadvert on another matter which seems to have puzzled – if not vexed – you? This concerns the attention which has been drawn to the nature of Watson's [*Blot!*] (These travelling ink-pots!) wound, which he received on the North West Frontier. You at least acknowledge that he referred to it sometimes as affecting his shoulder, and at others his leg, but are at a loss to account for this inconsistency.

I can assure you there is *no* inconsistency and, further, that he was not wounded on *two* occasions but only one. The fact is, as he himself explained to me, the Jezail bullet came from a sniper when he was in the act of pulling at his boot after getting his foot caught in a rocky fissure. He was, at that moment, completely doubled up and the bullet glanced off his ankle-bone nicking his Achilles tendon to pass beneath his collar-bone and lodge in his shoulder. He was thus shot in the front, not in the back, but the ludicrousness of his position has prevented his elaborating on a matter really quite irrelevant to his reports. It is even possible that the rocky fissure story may be just a euphemism for some more *fundamental* reason for being temporarily doubled up! If so, his reticence and your puzzlement are easily explained. (You will, I trust, keep this disclosure to yourself. Watson is somewhat sensitive on the subject and I feel I owe my information mainly to the mellow spirit of St Hogmanay!)

I understood that Watson's party were on a steep slope rising above a narrow hill-track, and that the bullet came *up* from some point below the track. The place was covered with boulders of all sizes and at first they feared an ambush, but no further shots followed. (At least, not while Murray was carrying Watson off.)

My kindest regards, and with the earnest wish that we may meet again as soon as I return from my native land (a final visit this time!) I particularly desire to discuss with you the intriguing question of Mr Mycroft Holmes's exact position in the Government. Is it true that he is officially known simply as 'M'?

Until we meet, I remain,
Yours sincerely,

MARCIUS TRAMPLE CLOISTURE

PS You remember Mr Morson, our senior partner? He has now retired and I expect a modest promotion after my holiday. If this happens we will celebrate at Mario's!

It is indeed fortunate that this missive has survived at all and we can only assume that it is what it appears to be – a chatty letter from a Mr Trample Cloisture to somebody called 'Arthur', whom he appears to have known at some time in Edinburgh. This can hardly be anybody but Arthur Conan Doyle, who studied medicine in Edinburgh, and Mr Cloisture may have been a fellow lodger or a chance acquaintance who became a close friend. He would seem to have come originally from some distant part of the Commonwealth or perhaps the USA, but he can hardly be a man of importance. Enquiries have been made at several of the Commonwealth offices, and at the American Embassy, but nobody seems to have heard of him. However, we do have a clue to the nature of his occupation and another to his actual place of business.

The first clue is the dirty red mark at the bottom of the third sheet, for an attempt to remove this was clearly made before the last two words were written, so that it could not have been acquired later, for example on the rubbish-tip. A small piece of it has been snipped off and subjected to expert examination; it is neither blood nor cocoa, but ferric oxide or jeweller's rouge! A spectroscopic test was confirmed by electron-probe analysis, and there can be no doubt about it. Mr Cloisture may therefore have been a jeweller, or in the habit of visiting a jeweller's workshop.

The second clue does more than support this supposition. There is a reference in the postcript to a 'Mr Morson, our senior partner,' and surely he can be none other than the head of Morson and Company, whose gem expert, Mr Purvis, was consulted in the matter of *The Jew's Breastplate*? This case was recounted by Watson's literary agent in his 'Tales of Mystery', but unfortunately Morson and Company no longer exist, their premises and records having presumably been destroyed during the Second World War.

Whoever Mr Cloisture's employers may have been, internal evidence in his letter encourages us to believe that it is genuine, for who would wish to forge such a letter from such a man? The fact that its writer nearly always uses Greek 'e's but occasionally writes Roman ones is of no significance. Handwriting is often very inconsistent in such details and, as it happens, Conan Doyle's writing shows the same peculiarity though his style is quite different. The writer's claim to be writing in a train is corroborated by the patches of scribble as it passed over points and crossings, and exceptionally clear passages when the train stopped at stations. And surely the very last place a forger would choose for his practice is a moving train!

It may be wondered how anybody (of the male sex) could come to spill rouge in a train, but this is not necessarily what happened. It is much more likely that Mr Cloisture's writing-pad was also the note-pad he used at his place of business and that the rouge got on to the paper there. When spilt, rouge is a most difficult substance to clean up and always leaves a stain on anything absorbent.

Again, the excellent preservation of the ink in which the letter is written has been shown by analysis with ultra-violet light to be due to its being the sort of carbon ink used for writing small code marks on specimens of ores and uncut stones, and not the common 'iron-gall' writing ink of the period. Since he carried such ink with him we may suppose Mr Cloisture to be a travelling buyer for his firm. It is true that Conan Doyle does not refer to him by name in his surviving writings (either private or published), but there must be scores of people whom he would have called his friends but never had occasion to mention.

Nevertheless, the name 'Marcius Trample Cloisture' has been regarded with suspicion by more than one critic.* Some have even regarded it as evidence of fraud, but surely not even a collector of old bottles would go to such lengths just to secure a snack in a pub! To put an end to all such speculation we have undertaken a modest investigation into the origins of this admittedly curious name and have found records of it, or of names much like it, as far back as Norman times. It is cognate with the Early French *closture,* closure, or perhaps *cloistre,* cloister, and on occasion it referred to a brotherhood of mendicant friars who came originally from a monastery founded by St Mark in Alexandria. Trample, of course, is Middle English for to walk heavily, and one can picture a column of mendicant friars plodding slowly along the streets of Alexandria – the trampers from St Mark's cloisters having an exclusive right to beg alms. No doubt the particular combination of names, Marcius Trample Cloisture, has appeared, vanished, and reappeared, sometimes with variations, often enough since the Middle Ages, and there is said to have been a quack known as Dr Tramper Closture selling nostrums in the south aisle of Old St Paul's in Charles I's time.

We may note, finally, that Mr Cloisture was an educated man though there were limits to his general knowledge. He writes 'your services to Watson should not prevent *your* trying your own hand . . .' – not 'you'.

* But the reader will find many much odder ones in the country's telephone directories and voting lists – Gompertz Jagelman, for example, or Trampleasure, Kneebone, Stinghorn, Eighteen, Stallybrass, Thicknesse.

And again, 'the ludicrousness of his position prevented *his* elaborating . . .' – not 'him'. But though these particularities suggest an education above the average, they might not have seemed so extraordinary at the time the letter was written, for English was then being properly taught in all schools.

But he writes 'Jezail' with a capital initial, as though he thought it the name of a tribe instead of merely a kind of musket, and his anatomical account of Watson's wound is not as precise as we could wish. The most plausible interpretation of it is illustrated in figure 10.

Fig. 10. How Dr Watson received his double wound at Maiwand, according to Mr Trample Cloisture.

It certainly looks as if the lung would have been punctured, but it is, perhaps, unfair to expect him to have thoroughly understood the doctor's description which was given under the influence of 'St Hogmanay'! Moreover, there is always the possibility that when Watson said that the bullet 'shattered the bone' he did not mean the shoulder-blade but the collar-bone. Elsewhere, Watson said he had had a jezail bullet *through* his leg, so that when he later referred to the bullet 'which I had brought back in one of my limbs' it would be a mistake to suppose him guilty of using the word 'limb' as a prudish euphemism for 'leg'. In fact, his ability to forget his 'game leg' (even in damp weather on Dartmoor) suggests that the bullet had not lodged in a nether limb but in the shoulder-joint of his left arm. Here, it could have 'shattered' the acromial end of the collar-bone and caused a splinter to graze the third part of the subclavian artery. This could certainly be said to affect one of his 'limbs', but there are too many possibilities to warrant further speculation.

7
The Case of the Cases

WE can hardly expect a general discussion of Sherlock Holmes's cases to be other than desultory and inconclusive, for we have too few hard facts and figures and too much information of doubtful relevancy or accuracy. Nevertheless, several quite remarkable features obtrude themselves on our attention almost at the outset. One of these is the enormous number of cases Holmes was able to handle.

In 1891, in *The Final Problem,* Holmes himself said, 'In over a thousand cases I am not aware that I have ever used my powers upon the wrong side.' He had then been practising for seventeen years, so that his average through that time was at least one case per week, with no holidays. Since many of the cases Watson has reported required some weeks for their completion, we may wonder how he could have maintained such an average. But this does not seem such a problem when we listen to Holmes's own description of his business.

When Watson first met him, Holmes said, 'I'm a consulting detective. . . . Here in London we have lots of Government detectives and lots of private ones. When these fellows are at fault, they come to me, and I manage to put them on the right scent. . . . I listen to their story, they listen to my comments, and then I pocket my fee.' And again, 'I examine the data, as an expert, and pronounce a specialist's opinion.' Such consultations may have required only a few hours each, and it was only 'now and again' that 'a case turns up which is a little more complex. Then I have to bustle about and see things with my own eyes.'

Thus, we can well understand what he means when, in *A Case of Identity*, he answers Watson's question, 'And have you any [cases] on hand just now?' with 'Some ten or twelve, but none which presents any feature of interest.' If he could handle ten or twelve cases at the same time it is unlikely that he had to do more than consult his Index and exercise his deductive powers. He might have had no more need to leave his room than Mycroft Holmes had when he amused himself with some of Sherlock's problems, and if only fifty per cent of his cases were as easily dealt with, his rate of work might have been only one case per fortnight; but we shall see that this must certainly be an underestimate.

However, even when he had to go out and see things with his own eyes, he often completed a case in a day or two. In *A Study in Scarlet* he points out to Watson, 'I was able to lay my hand upon the criminal within three days.' In *The Dying Detective* four days sufficed and it was the criminal, not Holmes, who went out to see things with his own eyes. On other occasions, it is true, his cases dragged on for weeks or months, or involved trips abroad, and these would tend to cancel out the gains achieved by his quick consultations. Nevertheless, when a case was temporarily held up the time of the delay was not necessarily wasted. He would still have had consultations to attend to, or details of other cases to follow up.

This was not, of course, always so. 'Day succeeded

day, and my friend took no step forward,' wrote Watson in *Wisteria Lodge,* and this time Holmes really was at a loose end. He complained, 'My mind is like a racing engine, tearing itself to pieces because it is not connected up with the work for which it was built. . . . Can you ask me, then, whether I am ready to look into any new problem, however trivial it may prove?' And in *The Copper Beeches* he was held up for lack of information for a fortnight and presently burst out with, 'Data! data! data! . . . I can't make bricks without clay.' The usual saying, based on the demands of the Egyptian taskmasters (in the book of *Exodus*), is 'you can't make bricks without straw,' but Holmes, with his usual perspicacity, saw that the clay is even more important. Straw was more useful for staging false alarms of 'Fire!', as in *The Norwood Builder.*

The case of *The Speckled Band* occurred in 1883, but Watson was not free to write it up until after the death of Miss Helen Stoner in 1891, eight years later. During those eight years he says he studied 'seventy odd cases'. He probably means more than seventy cases, though he omits the hyphen and so leaves 'odd' to describe the cases. Well, some of them were just that, for they included *The Man With the Twisted Lip, A Case of Identity*, and *The Yellow Face* – all certainly odd and needing no stronger epithet. But seventy cases in eight years means an average of only one every five weeks, and of these Watson reported more than twenty in full, mentioning incidentally about forty others. But there were certainly a great many more cases than these for, in 1889, in his account of *The Abbey Grange*, Watson said that he had notes of hundreds of cases to which he had never even alluded.

All things considered, it seems likely enough that his

average through those first seventeen years was about one case in eight or ten days, but there might be as many as a dozen in a single week or as few as one in a month. In 1891 Holmes left England for three years, but on his return in February 1894, he was immediately on call again, for Watson's notes of his cases during the remaining ten months of that year filled 'three massive manuscript volumes'. From these, Watson said he found it very difficult 'to select the cases which are most interesting in themselves and at the same time most conducive to a display of those peculiar powers for which my friend was famous.'

At the rate of one case every eight days Holmes would have dealt with about forty cases in those ten months, yet Watson reports only two, according to Baring-Gould, or five according to Martin Dakin. So his difficulty in selecting suitable cases was not because there were so many of them but because there were so few of interest. However, he mentioned some half a dozen others which may have been border-line cases (from his point of view).

In *The Solitary Cyclist* Watson said that 'From the years 1894 to 1901, inclusive, Mr Sherlock Holmes was a very busy man. It is safe to say that there was no public case of any difficulty in which he was not consulted during those eight years, and there were hundreds of private cases, some of them of the most intricate and extraordinary character, in which he played a prominent part.' Watson described twenty of these cases in full and referred to nineteen others. For this period an average rate at least as high as one case per week would seem plausible, though there were great irregularities.

For example, there was a temporary lapse of business in the second and third years after his return, for in 1895, the year of *The Norwood Builder,* after admitting that 'the community is certainly the gainer' by the death of Professor Moriarty, he adds, 'and no one the loser, save the poor out-of-work specialist, whose occupation has gone.' And in 1896, in the case of *The Missing Three-quarter,* he remarked, 'Even the most insignificant problem would be welcome in these stagnant days.'

Most of those 'hundreds of private cases', then, must have been crowded into the next three years, for again in 1901, in the case of *Thor Bridge,* he was saying, 'Yes, I have a case. After a month of trivialities and stagnation the wheels move once more.' Watson records only three cases for 1896 and two for 1901, though elsewhere he mentions two others which probably belong to 1901. In such slack times Watson probably took the opportunity to write up past cases from his notes. It was in 1896 that he referred to the 'long row of year-books which fill a shelf, and there are the dispatch-cases filled with documents.' His use of these must have entailed a great deal of care and consideration, for they evidently included the records of many delicate matters; he deprecated 'in the strongest way the attempts which have been made lately to get at and to destroy those papers.'

There are liable to be difficulties in placing in their correct order the various expressions of opinion recorded by Watson, for he may not have written them when they were spoken, or have published them when they were written. Some of his accounts are much too involved to have been remembered for long with any accuracy of detail, merely from notes jotted down at the time, so they were probably fairly completely written up soon after the events occurred. But publication was often deferred for many years – even decades, as Watson hints in *The Second Stain* – and then no doubt they underwent some preparation for the press. Martin Dakin (in *A Sherlock Holmes Commentary*) has shown that Watson sometimes transferred 'incidents and sayings, for literary effect, from their original contexts,' and, we may add, occasionally repeated them. Further, the stories were not by any means published in the order in which the cases occurred, so that we can only guess at the true chronology of Holmes's reported remarks.

As an example of the problems that are liable to arise, Watson says, in *The Devil's Foot,* that Holmes's objection to publicity was so strong that 'of late years' he had laid very few of his records before the public. Yet, in the same story, he reports Holmes as saying, with obvious encouragement, 'Why not tell them of the Cornish horror – the strangest case I have handled?' This case took place in 1897 but the account was not published until 1908, and there is no way of telling to which date either of these two attitudes of Holmes belongs.

In Watson's account of *Thor Bridge* Holmes said, 'I prefer to work anonymously' – an impossibility if taken literally, unless he was wearing a disguise. He was obviously referring to the published reports of his work, and in 1890, when *The Sign of Four* was published, Watson reports him as saying, 'My name figures in no newspaper.' But did that include *The Strand* magazine? It certainly included the magazine to which he contributed the article called *The Book of Life* for Watson had no idea who its author was when he read it (in *A Study in Scarlet*).

Yet, in 1897 again, after Holmes had complained of Watson's treatment of his cases, and Watson had retorted, 'Why do you not write them yourself?', Holmes replied, 'I will, my dear Watson, I will.' We have one or two examples of his efforts, and notably *The Blanched Soldier,* which Holmes wrote under his own name and in the first person! *The Blanched Soldier* affair has been dated at 1903, so it was written after his retirement, and we have seen that Holmes had certainly changed his mind before 1908. On the other hand, Martin Dakin may be right in supposing this story to be entirely spurious.

That Holmes, like most people, 'had his ups and downs' in this and other matters may seem a facile comment, but it is probably true enough. He was twenty-four when he set up shop in Montague Street, and fifty when he retired to keep bees in Sussex. In such a period his ideas are likely enough to have run through several phases, some of them even contradictory. One thing is certain, he was always absolutely devoted to his work and paid little serious attention to such side-effects as his personal reputation. In short, he liked his methods and their successful results to be publicized for their educational value, and did not wish to have them thought dependent for their success on some particular individual (himself).

'If I claim full justice for my art,' he is reported as saying in *The Copper Beeches*, 'it is because it is an impersonal thing – a thing beyond myself. Therefore it is upon the logic rather than upon the crime that you should dwell.' He then told Watson bluntly, 'You have degraded what should have been a course of lectures into a series of tales.' And, in *The Sign of Four,* he said, 'I claim no credit in such cases. . . . The work itself, the pleasure of finding a field for my peculiar powers, is my highest reward.'

Nevertheless, he was sometimes pleased to accept his fees, especially when they were 'princely', such as a cheque for £6,000 (or was it £12,000?) in *The Priory School,* or such gifts as gold snuff boxes and emerald tie-pins. But even here, he seems to have prized a photograph of Irene Adler above everything else. He also valued appreciation of his more remarkable feats, often announcing his success with some dramatic gesture, as in *The Naval Treaty, The Six Napoleons,* and *The Mazarin Stone.* His dramatic announcement at the climax of *The Man With the Twisted Lip,* 'Let me introduce you to Mr Neville St Clair, of Lee, in the county of Kent!' was a crow of triumph, but for the success of the investigation rather than for personal applause. 'To his sombre and cynical spirit all popular applause was always abhorrent,' wrote Watson – a remark in which the word 'always' relieves us from having to find a date for it.

'Nothing amused him more at the end of a successful case,' wrote Watson again, 'than to hand over the actual exposure to some orthodox official, and to listen with a mocking smile to the general chorus of misplaced congratulations.' 'Out of my last fifty-three cases,' said Holmes in *The Naval Treaty*, 'my name has only appeared in four, and the police have had all the credit in forty-nine.'

He preferred grotesque or bizarre problems to straightforward crimes and, in *Black Peter,* Watson notes that 'he frequently refused his help to the powerful and wealthy where the problem made no appeal to his sympathies, while he would devote weeks of intense application to the affairs of some humble client whose case presented those strange and dramatic qualities which appealed to his imagination and challenged his ingenuity.' And again, Watson said in *The Speckled Band* that 'he refused to associate himself with any investigation which did not tend towards the unusual, and even the fantastic.'

The cases which Watson has recounted cover a surprising variety of problems, yet only fourteen of the fifty-seven he wrote can really be called 'grotesque' or 'bizarre'. Ten are concerned with family problems or resolving delicate situations, and no less than nineteen do not even involve a crime (though seven of these are certainly unusual). These statistics are surprising in view of the truly enormous quantity of information to which Watson had access, though his sources, which we shall now summarize, are not free from problems of their own.

'When one considers that Mr Sherlock Holmes was in active practice for twenty-three years,' remarked Watson in his account of *The Veiled Lodger,* 'and that during seventeen of these I was allowed to co-operate with him and to keep notes of his doings, it will be clear that I have a mass of material at my command.' The major part, if not the whole, of this material was enshrined in the three massive manuscript volumes, the long row of year-books, the dispatch-cases filled with documents, and two other, separate tin boxes. The year-books would have been Holmes's professional records, and one of the tin boxes was also his. Though large, this was already in 1879 'a third full of bundles of paper tied up with red tape into separate packages. . . . "There are cases enough here Watson,"' Holmes said, and Watson guessed correctly that they were the records of his early work.

The other tin box was Watson's own private dispatch-box, old, much-travelled and battered, and inscribed

'John H. Watson, MD, Late Indian Army.' He says that it was crammed with papers, 'nearly all of which are records of cases to illustrate the curious problems which Mr Sherlock Holmes had at various times to examine.' That this box was not one of those 'dispatch-cases filled with documents' which Watson referred to in *The Veiled Lodger* as 'a perfect quarry for the student' is clear from the fact that he wrote these words sometime after 1921, and in *Thor Bridge,* published in 1922, he declared that his private dispatch-box had been stowed away in the vaults of the bank of Cox & Co. at Charing Cross – originally, we may suppose, for safe keeping during the First World War.

Watson tells us that it contained a number of the cases which Holmes had failed to solve, and this is, perhaps, one reason why it was left in the vaults at the bank and was not considered a particularly useful source of copy for publication. Watson (in *Thor Bridge*) mentions three examples of these 'unfinished tales': 'that of Mr James Phillimore, who, stepping back into his own house to get his umbrella, was never more seen in this world'; 'that of the cutter *Alicia,* which sailed one spring morning into a small patch of mist from where she never again emerged'; and 'that of Isadora Persano . . . who was found stark staring mad with a match-box in front of him which contained a remarkable worm, said to be unknown to science.' Watson then goes on to say, 'Apart from these unfathomed cases, there are some which involve the secrets of private families to an extent which would mean consternation . . . if it were thought possible that they might find their way into print.' It cannot really be credited that this collection was ever considered suitable for public quarrying by students of any age.

As for Holmes's private box of his early work, this had, no doubt, accompanied him down to Sussex. It was not something he would leave lying around and it is most unlikely that he would have given it to Watson. Had he done so, Watson would certainly have told us.

Of Holmes's thousand-odd cases, Watson mentioned only one hundred and forty, which is possibly ten per cent. He gave full accounts of less than half of these, in fact of only about four per cent of the total.

When Holmes had retired, he expressed a strong wish that Watson would not continue to publish his cases. In the opening paragraphs of *The Second Stain,* which were written in 1904, the year after Holmes's retirement, Watson said,

> I had intended the 'Adventure of the Abbey Grange' to be the last of those exploits of my friend Mr Sherlock Holmes, which I should ever communicate to the public. This resolution of mine was not due to any lack of material. . . . The real reason lay in the reluctance which Mr Holmes has shown to the continued publication of his experiences . . . notoriety has become hateful to him, and he has peremptorily requested that his wishes in this matter should be strictly observed.

But we have already cited evidence that he soon changed his mind and Watson subsequently published some twenty more of the hundred of cases of which he had records.

Holmes had often made clear his reasons for objecting to Watson's presentation of his cases, and Watson has frankly reported them. In *The Sign of Four,* he tells us, Holmes said,

> Detection is, or ought to be, an exact science . . . and should be treated in the same cold and unemotional manner. You have attempted to tinge it with romanticism, which produces much the same effect as if you worked a love-story or an

elopement into the fifth proposition of Euclid. . . . The only point in the case which deserves mention was the curious analytical reasoning from effects to causes, by which I succeeded in unravelling it. (The case referred to was *A Study in Scarlet*.)

Or again, in *The Crooked Man*, 'The effect of some of these little sketches of yours . . . is entirely meretricious,' and in *The Abbey Grange*, 'Your fatal habit of looking at everything from the point of view of a story instead of as a scientific exercise has ruined what might have been an instructive and even classical series of demonstrations. You slur over work of the utmost finesse and delicacy in order to dwell upon sensational details which may excite but cannot possibly instruct
Watson was, nevertheless, trying very hard to exhibit
the reader.'
Holmes's remarkable powers, and he actually stated that this was the chief point of his stories. He said, in *The Five Orange Pips*, that some of the cases 'have gained publicity through the papers, and others have not offered a field for those peculiar qualities which my friend possessed in so high a degree, and which it is the object of these papers to illustrate.'

Some of the cases which Watson would have liked to record he rejected because Holmes failed to display his special skill in them, and when he did venture to write them up, Holmes was liable to make such remarks as, 'In avoiding the sensational, I fear that you may have bordered on the trivial.' To do Watson justice, nearly all his reports were of Holmes's successes. He wrote, in *The Yellow Face*, 'In publishing these short sketches, based upon the numerous cases which my companion's singular gifts have made me the listener to . . . it is only natural that I should dwell rather upon his successes than upon his failures.' Perhaps this is what Holmes had in mind when he said, 'I must admit, Watson, that you have some power of selection which atones for much which I deplore in your narratives.'

Holmes was sometimes given to this sort of *double entendre*, as in his criticism of Watson's very first report, called *A Study in Scarlet.* 'I glanced over it,' said Holmes. 'Honestly, I cannot congratulate you upon it.' This was followed by the quotation on pages 119–120, but it was Holmes's first attack on Watson's writing and may have been said partly as a riposte to Watson's criticism of Holmes's own literary work, the article entitled *The Book of Life.* 'What ineffable twaddle!' Watson had said. 'I never read such rubbish in my life!' But that Holmes was also serious is evident from his later repeated criticisms.

In spite of this, however, he clearly did sometimes appreciate Watson's literary efforts as well as his selection of subjects. 'A good many of the criminal classes begin to know me,' he remarked, without rancour, to Athelney Jones in *The Sign of Four,* 'especially since our friend here took to publishing some of my cases.' In *A Scandal in Bohemia* Holmes said, 'you are good enough to chronicle one or two of my trifling experiences,' and Watson was so pleased with this that he made Holmes say it again in *A Case of Identity*: 'you, who have been good enough to chronicle one or two of my little problems.' In *The Dancing Men,* Watson reported Holmes as saying, 'you will have a very pretty case to add to your collection,' rubbing it in at the end of the case with, 'I have fulfilled my promise of giving you something unusual for your note-book.'

Referring to Stanley Hopkins in another case, Holmes remarked with apparent satisfaction, 'Hopkins has called me in seven times . . . I fancy that every one of his cases has found its way into your collection.' He even seemed to show apprehension when, as reported at the beginning of *The Stockbroker's Clerk,* he asked, 'I trust that you don't consider your collection closed?' But here, once again, he had a double motive, for what he really wanted this time was Watson's company on another investigation.

That he valued Watson's comradeship he stated very clearly some years later: 'A confederate who foresees your conclusions and course of action is always dangerous, but one to whom each development comes as a perpetual surprise, and to whom the future is always a closed book, is, indeed, an ideal helpmate.' So that, in view of his harsh criticisms of Watson's writing, it might be supposed that the various encouragements to add to his 'collection' were designed chiefly to secure his companionship. In *A Scandal in Bohemia* Holmes said, 'This is my friend and colleague, Dr Watson, who is occasionally good enough to help me in my cases' and, in *The Boscombe Valley Mystery,* 'It is really very good of you to come, Watson. . . . It makes a considerable difference to me, having someone with me on whom I can thoroughly rely.'

On the other hand, the reverse may be true: perhaps Holmes did take Watson along for the sake of the publicity which usually resulted. In *A Scandal in Bohemia* (again) Holmes said, 'I am lost without my Boswell' – not 'I am lost without my assistant.' Not only does Holmes refer to Watson as his faithful biographer, but he often seems to regard Watson's actual assistance in his cases as worse than useless, the only point in his favour being his possession of a revolver. Watson needed no encouragement to join in the adventures, but when he actually lent a hand he was seldom thanked for the effort. The following are but a few examples of Holmes's style of appreciation:

'Well, Watson . . . a pretty hash you have made of it . . . I cannot at the moment recall any possible blunder which you have omitted. The total effect of your proceedings has been to give the alarm everywhere and yet to discover nothing.' (*Lady Frances Carfax.*)

'Your hiding-place, my dear Watson, was very faulty. . . . You really have done remarkably badly.' (*The Solitary Cyclist.*)

'It is true that though in your mission you have missed everything of importance, yet even those things which have obtruded themselves upon your notice give rise to serious thought. . . . Clearly you have missed some vital points.' (*The Retired Colourman*, but Watson is then given a single word of praise – 'Excellent!' – because the number on a theatre ticket happened to be the same as his old school number, which 'stuck in my head'.)

There are, however, exceptions to this ungracious acknowledgement of Watson's efforts and, in fairness, we cite two. Watson was eminently successful in getting Mr Culverton Smith to attend the 'dying' detective and, afterwards, in becoming a witness to his confessions, and Holmes was obviously very grateful: 'My dear Watson, I owe you a thousand apologies. To think that I should have overlooked you!' And of Watson's full and painstaking reports from Baskerville Hall Holmes said: 'I must compliment you exceedingly upon the zeal and the intelligence which you have shown over an extraordinarily difficult case.'

But Watson's forte was, nevertheless, in action rather than thought and he saved Holmes's life more than once. When Watson was not grappling with somebody or assisting in a 'breaking-and-entering', Holmes was apt to use him as a blind if willing tool. When Holmes created a diversion by deliberately upsetting a table in *The Reigate Squires,* crying, 'You've done it now, Watson. . . . A pretty mess you've made of the carpet,' Watson at once accepted the situation, though with some confusion, and played up admirably. A few minutes later he was grappling with Alec Cunningham and saving Holmes's life.

Watson made no complaint at being sent off to Little Purlington with Mr Amberley, that detestable retired colourman, where they were forced to spend the night at the village inn, even though he was not told why he should go. But Holmes certainly valued Watson for other reasons than that he could be so used without question or complaint. His moral support was always welcome and, among his other qualities, he always had 'his feet on the ground' and was a steady influence. 'Good old Watson!' was 'the one fixed point in a changing age.' In short, he was good ballast and thoroughly dependable (except when he ignored Holmes's request for a description of Dr Shlessinger's left ear).

Their companionship seems to have been a marriage of opposites, for they were certainly devoted to one another – Watson rather like a faithful dog and Holmes like its master. Though Holmes was the reticent, unemotional, outwardly cold partner, it was he and not Watson who gave voice to his affection on at least two occasions. He expressed touching concern when Watson fainted 'for the first and last time in my life' at Holmes's sudden appearance in London after being presumed dead for three years. 'My dear Watson . . . I owe you a thousand apologies. I had no idea you would be so affected.' And when, in *The Three Garridebs,* Killer Evans shot at Watson, Holmes cried, 'You're not hurt, Watson? For God's sake, say that you are not hurt!' Watson commented, 'It was worth a wound – it was worth many wounds – to know the depth of loyalty and love which lay behind that cold mask. The clear, hard eyes were dimmed for a moment, and the firm lips were shaking. For the one and only time I caught a glimpse of a great heart as well as a great brain.' Watson's reciprocal feeling is reflected in both the incidents.

Sherlock Holmes's observations on his cases in general amount to a philosophy, or at least to a set of principles. The following examples of his sayings in illustration of this need no comment, except to point out that the first two are not contradictory; Holmes escaped from the commonplaces by elucidating them.

My life is spent in one long effort to escape from the commonplaces of existence. These little problems help me to do so. *(A Case of Identity)*

Depend upon it there is nothing so unnatural as the commonplace. (ibid)

Singularity is almost invariably a clue. The more featureless and commonplace a crime is, the more difficult is it to bring it home. *(The Boscombe Valley Mystery)*

I play the game for the game's own sake. *(The Bruce-Partington Plans)*

What you do in this world is a matter of no consequence. . . . The question is, what can you make people believe that you have done. *(A Study in Scarlet)*

There is nothing more deceptive than an obvious fact. *(The Boscombe Valley Mystery)*

The larger crimes are apt to be the simpler, for the bigger the crime, the more obvious, as a rule, is the motive. *(A Case of Identity)*

It has long been an axiom of mine that the little things are infinitely the most important. (ibid)

Circumstantial evidence is a very tricky thing . . . it may seem to point very straight to one thing, but if you shift your own point of view a little, you may find it pointing in an equally uncompromising manner to something entirely different. *(The Boscombe Valley Mystery)*

It is an old maxim of mine that when you have excluded the impossible, whatever remains, however improbable, must be the truth. *(The Beryl Coronet)*

You will remember that I remarked the other day . . . that for strange effects and extraordinary combinations we must go to life itself, which is always far more daring than any effort of the imagination. *(The Red-Headed League)*

When you have four million human beings all jostling each other within the space of a few square miles . . . every possible combination of events may be expected to take place, and many a little problem will be presented which may be striking and bizarre without being criminal. *(The Blue Carbuncle)*

Life is infinitely stranger than anything which the mind of man could invent. We would not dare to conceive the things which are really mere commonplaces of existence. If we could fly out of that window hand in hand, hover over this great city, gently remove the roofs, and peep in at the queer things which are going on . . . it would make all fiction . . . most stale and unprofitable. *(A Case of Identity)*

Those last two quotations call to mind a passage in Carlyle's *Sartor Resartus*, where Herr Teufelsdröckh, Professor of Things in General, sits in his attic at the top of the highest house in Weissnichtwo, brooding over the sea of roofs and smoking chimneys visible from his four windows and wondering what was going on beneath them. His meditation went on into the night, but his thoughts were surely similar to those of Sherlock Holmes who, because he believed that a serious investigator should 'cut out the poetry', could not have expressed them nearly as effectively:

'Upwards of five-hundred-thousand two-legged animals without feathers lie round us, in horizontal positions; their heads all in nightcaps, and full of the foolishest dreams. Riot cries aloud, and staggers and swaggers in his rank dens of shame; and the Mother, with streaming hair, kneels over her pallid dying infant, whose cracked lips only her tears now moisten. – All these heaped and huddled together, with nothing but a little carpentry and masonry between them; – crammed in, like salted fish in their barrel; – or weltering, shall I say, like an Egyptian pitcher of tamed vipers, each struggling to get its *head above* the others: *such* work goes on under that smoke-counterpane! – But I, *mein Werther*, sit above it all; I am alone with the Stars.'

We looked in his face to see whether, in the utterance of such extraordinary Night-thoughts, no feeling might be traced there; but with the light we had, which indeed was only a single tallow-light, and far enough from the window, nothing save that old calmness and fixedness was visible.

Sherlock Holmes, however, did not remain aloof. He came down to earth at the knock of a possible client, or to rouse the still slumbering Watson with the urgent cry, 'The game is afoot! Not a word! Into your clothes and come!' Watson always came and if, as it chanced, they sped across country to engage in some strange rural adventure, Watson would be liable to comment on the charming 'little red roofs of the farm-steadings' and 'these dear old homesteads', saying with all the enthusiasm of a man fresh from the fogs of Baker Street, 'Are they not fresh and beautiful?' Holmes would then drop into his Teufelsdröckhian mood again with:

You look at these scattered houses, and you are impressed by their beauty. I look at them, and the only thought which comes to me is a feeling of their isolation, and of the impunity with which crime may be committed there. . . . They always fill me with a certain horror. . . . But look at these lonely houses, each in its own fields, filled for the most part with poor ignorant folk who know little of the law. Think of the deeds of hellish cruelty, the hidden wickedness which may go on, year in, year out, in such places, and none the wiser.

But Holmes was most at home in London, 'in the very centre of five millions of people', and we read that Herr Teufelsdröckh, too, was eventually drawn to that same, sprawling city, some twenty years before Holmes was born. He vanished mysteriously from Weissnichtwo but, says Carlyle (in editorial vein), 'Our own private conjecture, now amounting almost to certainty, is that, safe-moored in some stillest obscurity, not to lie always still, Teufelsdröckh is actually in London!'

But there is this difference: Teufelsdröckh did nothing for London, but Holmes, even by 1891, when he temporarily vanished, told Watson, 'I think that I may go so far as to say . . . that I have not lived wholly in vain. If my record were closed tonight I could still survey it with equanimity. The air of London is the sweeter for my presence.' For many people he is still there: the old bee-keeper in Sussex is just his *alter ego*, who got side-tracked in 1903.

Appendix

HOLMES'S ZOOLOGY

The following are the names of animals (and some of their young) referred to by Dr Watson in his records of Sherlock Holmes's cases. ('Medusa' is used instead of the poetic 'lion's mane'.)

VERTEBRATES

Mammals
Dog
Coyote
Donkey
Horse
Colt
Pony
Cattle
Oxen
Cow
Bullock
Buffalo
Stag
Pig
Boar
Cat
Lion
Tiger
Cheetah
Lynx
Bear
Camel
Baboon
Chimpanzee
Ape
Monkey
Langur
Sheep
Lamb
Goat
Kid
Badger
Weasel
Stoat
Ferret
Mongoose
Rat
Rabbit
Bat
Vampire
Mole
Seal
Whale

Reptiles
Snake
Cobra
'Swamp-adder'
Viper
Lizard
Slow-worm

Amphibians
Frog

Birds
Fowl
Cock
Hen
Goose
Duck
Dove
Pheasant
Woodcock
Owl
Sea-bird
Cormorant

Vulture	Buzzard	*Fishes*
Eagle	Canary	Pike
Bittern		Trout

INVERTEBRATES

Shrimp	Leech	Cockroach	Butterfly
Oyster	Worm	Beetle	Moth
Medusa	Spider	Fly	Bee

We must assume that Holmes was familiar with the appearance of most of these creatures, and with some of their habits and a few of their tracks, but there is no evidence that his zoological knowledge extended any further. Since he lived in Baker Street and sometimes took a stroll round Regent's Park it is possible that he visited the Zoo, but if in that way he ever gleaned any special knowledge of the exotic species he probably told Watson, 'Now that I do know it I shall do my best to forget it.' It was enough, for a consulting detective, to know that snakes are often poisonous, cheetahs and baboons are dangerous, and mongooses and monkeys are adept climbers. He could always consult the Encyclopaedia or the works of the Rev. J. G. Wood for special information on anthropoid apes or 'lion's manes'. Nevertheless, the list is quite a formidable one, containing, as it does, no less than seventy-eight names – 1·3 per story!

Index